AlphaGraphics,
788 Brookhaven Circle East
Memphis, TN 38117
www.us046.alphagraphics.com
Phone (901) 681-9909
Fax (901) 761-2139

The World Was Our Oyster Until!
Printed by: AlphaGraphics, Inc.
Is printed on biodegradable, renewable, recyclable and sustainable paper.
Forests clean the air we breathe.
It will help protect our forests and prevent their conversion to other uses.
It will protect jobs.
Paper is GOOD.

Copyright © 2021 J. Roscoe Phillips
Publidshed in the United States of America
All rights reserved

First Edition

ISBN 978-1-63848-042-6
The text in this book is composed in Palatino

Cover designed by J. Roscoe Phillips
Interior design and typesetting by J. Roscoe Phillips
Photos and illustrations by J. Roscoe Phillips

An introduction to our world of travel!

Here are many stories of our long distance trips by bicycle and the wonderful people we met. These are stories of people, places and travels from our beginning as a couple, to retirement, and to the end of our ability to travel long distances by bicycle. It is sad and difficult to admit the fun of long distance travel by bicycle is over.

I hope these stories will bring a smile to your face, and encourage you to find your own adventures as you travel through life.

There were many training rides, in order to have the ability to ride our bicycles 60 to 80 miles per day. During our travels we rode 119 miles in one day. Read about that part of our travels in "The World Was Our Oyster, Until!" The "Until" is related to the events of 9/11, when the world changed from a trusting life style to one of mistrust. With the many changes, it made traveling by bicycle difficult and very expensive to fly with a bicycle.

J. Roscoe & Ann M. Phillips

Dedication

This book and the many stories included in these pages really belong to the following people.

Ann McFarlan Phillips
Lewis O'Kelly of Memphis, TN
Charles Finney, Memphis, TN
Sid and Dot Cromwell of Murfreesboro, TN
Mr. Cordell Kemp of Defeated Creek, TN
Clay and Jan Simon of Mosier, OR
Sylvia Dahlberg and the Club Artist Group
of Vasteras, Sweden
Geraldine Jacobson of Hope, ND
Marian Kleweno, of Bazine, KS
Clovis Mott, of Centerville, MO
Robert D Sensenig of Rochester, NY
Betty and Dick Allen of Fairhope, AL
Betty and Virgil Bowles of Leesburg, FL
George & Lonny Parsons of Raton, NM

Much appreciation goes out to Dick Bevier for reading and rereading this book to help me with my editing, thank you.

The author at age 3 on his first wheeled vehicle.
J. Roscoe Phillips
Born at Dyess Colony, Arkansas

I always wanted to ride long distance on a bicycle. When I received my first two-wheeler, my mother insisted it was too far for me to ride to school, (three and a half miles), from our home. From that day, I always wanted to prove to her that I could ride anywhere on a bicycle. Before my mother's death, Ann, and I rode across the United States. After the ride we went to visit her just to say, "See, I could have ridden my bicycle to school." Ann and I have ridden our bicycles over 100,000 kilometers (63,000 plus miles) since 1999.

In the Beginning

In 1980, my father passed away at the age of 80. This does not sound like a bad age to die. He was the last male of his family to die, all of his brothers had passed away. It would appear he did something correctly and they had not. Well, that's how I felt that day at my father's funeral. I began to look around the room and realized all of his family had passed from this world except one sister and she was too sick to attend the funeral. My sisters and I were left to care for our mother, who didn't want our help.

I drove back to Little Rock, Arkansas alone and began to wonder about my own physical condition. I was getting fat. I was in need of a physical fitness program. This was in July and the weather was rather hot. I began a walk and jog program described in a Sports Illustrated handbook I'd purchased a few years earlier but had never touched. When your father, aunts, and uncles have all died of heart attacks, it is time to start, getting ready to have your own heart attack or to begin a fitness program and prevent it. I wanted to be in the best physical shape possible when I had my pending heart attack. I am still waiting and now I no longer look forward to having one as I've reached the age of eighty-four and it has not yet appeared.

In the evenings, I would jog at a nearby junior high track, join a large crowd of walkers and joggers for thirty minutes, and then return home with a renewed quest to continue this endeavor each day until I could run as well as two other men on the track about my age. I began to walk less and jog more and the jogging turned into running. I feel anything under an eight-minute mile is running.

I met Charles Ray and Edgar Evans at the track and we began to run together each afternoon. From the track we advanced to running on the road and then traveled to races around Arkansas. First we ran the 5K races and later the 10K races. I found a few races where I could win second or third place if Don Potter of Benton, Arkansas or Henry Hawk of Conway, Arkansas didn't show up to race or they attended another race on the same day. Most of the time the results were the same, I came in third place.

In 1984, I bought myself a first-class bicycle and began to train for biathlons (later changed to duathlons). I soon learned I could win first place by riding a bicycle and running and I love winning. This was my first taste of bicycling since my childhood. Things would change, as I changed jobs in 1987 and moved from Little Rock, Arkansas to Memphis, Tennessee. Since I didn't know anyone in Memphis and I worked nights, this combination gave me time to run and bicycle. First I met the Hash-House-Harriers. In case you don't know, they are billed as a "running club with a drinking problem" or a "drinking club with a running problem," whichever. They really have a great down-down at the end of each run. Second, I joined the Memphis Runners Club, and third I joined the Memphis Hightailers Bicycle Club. That was how I began to create my database of friends in Memphis.

In 1988, I rode the MS 150, a 150-mile bicycle ride to raise money for Multiple Sclerosis. The company where I was employed and my fellow workers raised over three hundred dollars toward my ride. I didn't let them down, as I rode all 150 miles. The ride was from Memphis to Reelfoot Lake State Park. The next year, 1989, the ride was from Memphis to Pickwick Landing State Park with an overnight stop in Jackson, Tennessee at Lambuth College and I signed up for the ride. Again the company and fellow workers came through with the required donations for me to make the ride, but this year another employee also signed up for the ride. A young man called Rusty, and he began to brag about how he would leave me in the dirt. It just happened that earlier, I had raced against John Groff in Huntsville, Alabama and as Rusty continued his bragging, John interrupted him and said "Rusty, that old man is going to hurt you bad." Well, John knew how competitive I was and how I had out bicycled and out run him in Huntsville and he knew I would do all I could to out ride Rusty. When we left State Tech parking lot on that Saturday morning in May, Rusty and I joined a fast pace line and twelve miles down the road Rusty stopped at the first rest stop. I didn't see him until late that evening. I had showered and dressed for dinner by the time he arrived. Yes, I had hurt Rusty badly.

    I was feeling great that evening and as we ate dinner the promoters began to give out awards for first in, in each age group. They asked for women 50 years and older and finally a lady raised her hand and was given the "first in" in the 50 and over age group. When she walked out of the building, I followed. Since I was over fifty and since she was very attractive and since I was single and since she was single, I thought it would be nice of me to let her know I was over fifty also.

    When I introduced myself and stated I was over fifty, all she said was, "Excuse me, but I am going for a walk." I returned to my dorm alone, wondering if she was attached or alone but what the heck, I had all day tomorrow to find out. When I entered the dorm I heard a gentleman state that he had asked the promoters why only the women over 50 were awarded a prize. He had also stated he was over fifty and the first male to arrive in Jackson. This was just too much. I introduced myself and stated that could not be as I was fifth in, in a pace line of eight riders who were first to arrive in Jackson. He said, "Well, this prize is yours but you won't ever beat me again." Since that time, Lowell Blakney has always come in in front of me in all the rides we have participated in together. In 2001 as we rode across North Carolina, he was first in, ahead of me every day of the seven-day ride. Lowell, lives in Counce, Tennessee and is one of the many bicyclists I call a friend.

On the second day of the ride to Pickwick Landing State Park from Jackson, Tennessee I was out early but not as fast as the day before, and sure enough Lowell did what he said, he came in ahead of me. I had plenty of time to think about the lady over fifty from the night before. I also had discovered her name, Ann Kimball. I formulated a plan to meet her at the end of the ride on Sunday. When she rode toward the finish line, I would have her bag and also welcome her with a loud applause. This I did, and then I introduced myself to her for a second time. Also, since I had arrived early I knew where the showers were located. I led the way to the showers. After the ride, we ate an early dinner and walked down to where the Bass Tournament weigh-in was taking place. We marveled over the size of the bass as each one weighed more than the one before. Then we loaded on a bus and I began to tell her all about myself. When we arrived back at the parking lot at State Tech I helped her load her bicycle onto her bike rack. When I picked it up, it weighed a ton, so I said "If you had had a decent bicycle you really could have come in first place after riding this bicycle for 150 miles." She was somewhat offended but then I had her pick up my bicycle and she was surprised by how light it was. Her daughter had purchased the bicycle for her mother thinking it would be for riding around the neighborhood. I didn't know how much I had impressed her, except to find out later, when she left the State Tech parking lot, to head home, she had driven north on Sycamore View instead of south toward Germantown.

I had explained to her on the bus how I worked nights and could ride a bicycle all day if she needed a riding partner. She did. We began to ride together. I found a quest, as we later began to describe our bicycle rides. The quest would lead us in search of Dr. John R. Brinkley's grave. Just in case you are asking who is Dr. John R. Brinkley? Well, he was the first transplant doctor. According to the Border Radio by Gene Fowler and Bill Crawford, "the 1920's were known for their extravagance, flappers and flaming youth. But what if the flame was running a little low? Dr. Brinkley had just the thing for you (males): transplant a few slivers of Randy, goat gonads into the woeful subject's scrotum and ta-dahh - rejuvenation! With this simple procedure, Dr. Brinkley built himself an empire, and in 1923, he began his infomercials - always laced with Biblical references - over KFKB, the first radio station in Kansas. More than 3,000 letters a day eventually started pouring into little Milford, KS, prompting Brinkley to finance a new post office. By 1929, KFKB had won a gold cup as the most popular radio station in America." I doubt that many readers realize that Dr. Brinkley is buried here in Memphis. Needing a reason for our bicycle rides, Ann and I rode to Elmwood Cemetery in search of Dr. Brinkley's grave. We searched without asking for help and when we had reached the end of our efforts we rode to the office to ask if they had a record of his burial. Now this is where all this was leading to, as we stood in the garden outside the office I leaned over from my bicycle to offer a kiss, it was accepted and we began a romance that has lasted for over thirty-two years and we hope for even more years to come.

Later that year, I proposed to Ann with a stipulation, I sell my house and purchase a share of hers. This was accepted and

I began to just ride along, without any effort to sell my house and in not too much of a hurry to finalize my commitment. Not so! Ann showed up with a real estate dealer, I signed a contract and the house sold in a week. Now I must stand good on my proposal. We do not have an engagement ring, I told her. Her answer, no problem everything will work out. Now, you may think this is cheap on my part or you may think I was a genius. I suggested we go to Arkansas and dig in the diamond fields of their state park and when we find a diamond it would become the stone for the engagement ring. Great plan? Well, I thought so, I created a sifter system, took the proper tools, a potato digger, and headed to Murfreesboro, Arkansas. We arrived just ahead of a gully washer. As we stood in the park headquarters, with my digging tools, Ann and I began to laugh about what we had brought to search for diamonds. Then as I looked around, a gentleman with a great southern voice said, "Well, boy, looks like you came to dig taters." I replied, "Oh no!" "We came for the big diamonds." He said, "Nope, you came to dig taters with that thing." Well, I suppose he was correct for the only thing we found was knee deep mud. We left the diamond fields with two pairs of shoes we could never wear again.

The engagement ring came just as Ann had predicted and we settled into the planning of getting married. We decided to ride across Tennessee in September for our honeymoon. This would be a ride sponsored by the Parks and Tourism Department of Tennessee with the acronym, BRAT, for Bike Ride Across Tennessee. We made reservations at all the state parks we would ride through and sat back to wait for the date to roll around. I worked nights and we played days. Then in August, Ann's daughter, Susan and her husband, Marty Hawkins, came home to visit for the last time before Susan would deliver a granddaughter for Ann in October.

It was a Thursday night at work when I received a phone call asking, "Roscoe, do you think we could get married this weekend? This is the last time Susan can travel in her condition and if we wait until September to marry she cannot return for the wedding." "Well I suppose we can, if you can find anyone who will marry us on such short notice." In a few minutes she called again and stated, "The minister has refused to marry us on such short notice." "Well Ann, we can find a judge to do the job and then later on have a minister perform the ceremony." She and I continued to discuss the situation and then she decided to make another call to the church to protest the decision by the senior pastor. Then another phone call to me and she said the associate pastor would marry us. We would have to apply for the license on Friday, meet with Frank Beck on Saturday and he would marry us on Sunday. We hurriedly made a list of people to call and planned a reception as well as a wedding. All of this was accomplished and on Sunday, August 20, 1989 at 2:30 p.m., we were married by Frank Beck, in the little chapel at Germantown Presbyterian Church. The wedding party consisted of seventeen people, three daughters, a friend of my daughter, a cousin, his wife and two sons, a son-in-law, his mother and sister, a best man and his date, Ann's mother, Ann and myself and of course Frank. The reception was held at the Adams Mark, Frank and my cousins didn't attend the reception, so we had a dozen people around us that afternoon at the Adams Mark. Then Ann and I jumped into my car and headed to the Peabody. This was the ultimate goal in my life, to stay at the Peabody someday and so we did just that. We spent our first night at the Peabody.

Let me tell how much I had looked forward to someday staying in the Peabody. I was born and grew up at Dyess Colony, Arkansas. Dyess had a Central Baptist Church and that is where I spent my Sundays, both morning and evening. The mornings were all right but evenings I would be so tired I always wanted to stay home. This did not happen. I had to attend. Now it was okay for me to fall asleep but I had to attend Sunday night service. So, I think I heard the preacher say that when we died, we would go to the Peabody. I'll never swear to this but I love to tell that we had a chance to go to the Peabody. Now this is August 20, 1989 and I am still alive and Ann and I are checking in to the Peabody for our first night as a married couple. We still had plans for our honeymoon in September.

BRAT 1989
The Delayed Honeymoon

We delayed our honeymoon until late September as we wanted to ride BRAT. This we did along with five hundred plus bicyclists. We started in Limestone, Tennessee, the birthplace of David Crockett and rode south and east across Tennessee to Tim's Ford State Park near Winchester. Sounds simple enough for two people whose love is bicycling, plus we had bought Ann a new Bianchi bicycle. Did I forget to mention that hurricane Hugo was playing havoc along the coast and coming north across Tennessee just as BRAT was starting across the state? Our first night we spent in a tent and didn't look forward to setting it up again on our ride. Everyone was wet and so, when we arrived at Panther Creek State Park and the others found out that we had a room at the local Holiday Inn, naturally they hinted that sleeping bags and a slumber party would be great. We acted as if we could not hear them, even with much moaning and groaning. We turned a deaf ear. This was our honeymoon and it was not anyone else's business that we were riding across Tennessee on a honeymoon. As the week wore on and the rain increased, so did the persistence from the other riders, that we share our rooms with them. Again, Ann and I turned a deaf ear. When we arrived at Fall Creek Falls State Park, the rain had increased even more and the temperature had dropped to almost freezing. We had a room at Neil's Motel, which looked a lot like the Bates Motel in "Psycho." It was located outside of the park by several miles. When we arrived, our luggage had been delivered and we were ready to shower and enjoy the warmth of our room. Wait a minute, it was just as cold inside the room as outside, the only thing different was it was dry inside. When I attempted to turn on the heat, the knob on the heater began to spin and probably is still spinning. I called the office and reported that we did not have any heat. The lady said just turn the knob, when I announced the knob was still spinning she said, "Oh! You have that room, if you will come to the office, we will loan you a space heater." At least we were dry, we never did get really warm that evening.

Along about Thursday some of the riders from Memphis had talked, and word began to spread that we were indeed on our honeymoon. The request to join us in our room turned from moans and groans to jokes about the honeymoon couple. Sid and Dot Cromwell from Murfreesboro, Tennessee, began to rib us at each stop along the way. As I stated earlier about bicycle friendships, Sid and Dot are counted among our dearest of bicycle friendships. We have ridden on a total of three BRAT rides and each time was with Sid and Dot.

After our rain-soaked honeymoon, Susan Hawkins presented a beautiful young lady as our first granddaughter. She is named Lillian after her great-grand mother and goes by Lilly. I had made an "honest grandmother" out of Ann, and just in time. Lilly was born in October, 1989. We have enjoyed her company one day a week for most of her life except when we were off on one of our quests.

Red Boiling Springs 1989
Ann and The Tobacco Crop

We are members of the Memphis Hightailers Bicycle Club. Each year the club sponsors a ride from Lebanon to Red Boiling Springs and back to Lebanon through Carthage, the hometown of Vice President Al Gore. The ride has been held in August in the past years in conjunction with the Medicine Man Show in Red Boiling Springs. The first year Ann and I did the ride, the tobacco crops of east Tennessee were just beginning to get ripe. Now Ann is an expert on crops and began to explain to me that the yellow fields had received too much rain and that was the reason the crops were turning yellow. This went on all day as we rode to Red Boiling Springs. The next day as we

Ann Phillips, Mr. Cordell Kemp, and Roscoe Phillips listening to Mr. Kemp play the banjo, and Roscoe faking playing the banjo.

were leaving the Cumberland Plateau, there is a great hill for letting it all hang out. Bicyclists have reached speeds of better than fifty-five miles per hour. Near the end of this great run off is the town of Defeated Creek. As Ann and I entered Defeated Creek, a farmer called out, "You are number twenty-five, you are number twenty-six." I flagged Ann to stop and explained that this was the farmer to ask about his tobacco, because all he has to do today is count bicycles. We turned around and rode into his yard. I explained that we needed some information about his tobacco crop, he asked "Are you cutters?" "No, we aren't cutters, but my wife is from New Jersey and noticed that your crop is turning yellow and was sure it had received too much rain and was beginning to spoil." He replied, "No," "Boy it's ripe and I need cutters. I'll put you to work in the morning if'n you're cutters." "No," "We'll have to pass, but thanks for the information" I responded. As we began to turn around he said, "Boy, you don't know whose yard you rode into do you?" "No sir, I don't," I said. "Well, let me introduce myself, I'm Mr. Cordell Kemp, I'm the man who taught Uncle Dave Megan how to play the banjo. How would you like to hear me play the banjo?" "We'd love to," I said, as we stopped in our tracks. He reached behind him and pulled out his banjo and began to play. As other bicyclists came down off the Cumberland Plateau, saw us in his yard and heard his music, they also stopped. This was really a great treat and a day it didn't pay to be a fast bicyclists for Mr. Kemp would have played all night if we had stayed in his yard to listen.

That was in 1990. In 1991, Ann and I were riding BRAT for the second time. When we arrived in Edgar Evins State Park, there was very little space to set up our tent and very little flat area for camping. The tents were set up against each other. We were tired and exhausted, so we decided to avoid the nightly entertainment. We went to bed early but the stage was just too close to avoid the sound system. The announcer said, "Ladies and gentlemen, the entertainment tonight is the man who taught Uncle Dave Megan how to play the banjo, Mr. Cordell Kemp." Of course, we had to crawl out of the tent and attend the entertainment. I walked over to the stagehand and explained how we had met him last year on a bicycle ride through Defeated Creek. The stagehand said, "After this number, just walk out on the stage, he'll remember you." Well, sure, I thought, Mr. Kemp appears to be close to two hundred years old and he would remember me. I began to walk out on the stage and he looked up as I said, "Mr. Kemp, I don't know if you remember me or not." He said "Course I do boy; you're married to that little old Yankee girl." This brought down the house and a big smile from Ann. I asked him if he needed cutters and he replied, "Boy, I need strippers, the tobacco is in the barn."

There are those who drive past Mr. Kemp's house in Defeated Creek and never notice him sitting on his porch. I don't believe Mr. Kemp would ever count cars, and if so, how many drivers would ever hear him when he called out their number as they drove through Defeated Creek. We did, because we were on bicycles and riding quietly along listening to the sounds of the day, when Mr. Kemp called out the numbers for our bicycles.

That night with the tents so close together everyone could hear their neighbor and all the sounds of the night. Snoring is one thing Ann cannot stand, nor will she let me indulge in such a pleasure. Do you think she would let our neighbor get away with snoring all night? Not on your life! When she had had all she could stand, she crawled out of the tent and grabbed his tent, shook it firmly and shouted, "rollover." I suppose he did for we didn't hear from him the rest of the night and all the tents around us roared in great approval at Ann's action.

We have ridden three BRAT rides but none will ever equal the Hugo ride of 1989, and none will ever treat us to the great entertainment we received in 1991 when Mr. Kemp played his banjo just for Ann and me. We also rode BRAT in 1993, from Bristol, to Chattanooga. Tennessee has fifty-five state parks and Ann and I have ridden to most of them on our bicycles.

Our First Great Quest
1990 Cycle America Across Washington State

When the time rolled around for a vacation, we had decided to ride across America, one state at a time. We would start with Washington and work our way east from one state to the other with Cycle America. This sounds easy enough, except, we started with the hardest state to ride across. There are the Cascade Mountains and rain in Washington. We departed Anacortes, Washington in the rain and by the time we reached Newport, Washington, both of us had a deep cough and pain in our backs. I knew we had pneumonia. On our ride across Washington, we climbed from 900 feet above sea level to 5,477 feet on our second day. This is a forty-eight-mile continuous grade, the longest continuous grade in the state of Washington. On this day we rode over Washington Pass at 5,477 feet and that evening my right leg was in such pain, I had to pull up short of our campground in Winthrop. I had to accept a ride into camp. I was sure my knee was out for the rest of the week. One of the riders was a veterinarian, and began to tell me about a medicine that was approved only for horses in the United States, but was approved for humans in Canada, and how it would work on my leg if I wanted her to spray my knee, she would do so. I really felt I had little choice, and I allowed her to spray my knee with what I now know to be DMSO. I have never had another problem with that knee. I occasionally wake up nights pawing the bed as if counting with my hoofs and Ann says that I disturb her when I whiney like a horse in my sleep, but other than that I have never had any ill effects.

The third day we turned south from Winthrop, out of the rain and rode 109 miles to Grand Coulee Dam. On day four, we returned to the rain zone, at the foot of Sherman Pass and checked into a motel in Republic, rather than camp. We were cold, wet and tired from the long ride north. We asked for a room with a large tub and to our surprise we were given the handicap room, large tub, you bet. After this surprise I inquired about a good local restaurant and was told, there was a gourmet restaurant across the street from the motel. Gourmet! Sure, in Republic, Washington, we could see from one side of town to the other and they have a gourmet restaurant? Believe me, they do have a gourmet restaurant in Republic. Ann and I enjoyed a great dinner of Steak Oscar and a supreme bottle of wine to celebrate four days of bicycling in Washington state.

In Colville, we were welcomed into town by Miss Colville and her princesses and were featured in their local newspaper. Everyone we met along the way was impressed that we were riding a bicycle across Washington. When we explained, there were others who planned to ride across the U.S.A. they really looked at us as if we had lost it all, or didn't have it to begin with. Our coughs had begun in earnest by this time and neither of us felt strong but we wouldn't give up for anything.

When we reached Newport, Washington it was Grizzly Days and a 5K race would be held the next morning. I was determined to run in the race. The Newport Grizzly Run, I won third place in my age group and felt I had accomplished the very best I could that day. The next day we flew home from Spokane.

When we arrived back home, we headed for the doctor's office and sure enough, Ann had pneumonia in her right lung and I had pneumonia in my left lung and Dr. John Buttross gave us two choices, to the hospital or home with bed rest for nine days. We opted for home and stuck to it because he made sure we understood how serious our condition really had become. This was our first ride with Cycle America. We have ridden several other rides with them since 1990.

We rode from Montpelier, Idaho to West Yellowstone, Montana and from Astoria, Oregon to Crescent City, California with Cycle America, but those are stories to write about further along in our quest for great adventures.

Sid and Dot Cromwell
Tennessee 1989-2001
Let's Go Self-Contained!

Once we had recovered from pneumonia, we began to ride closer to our home in Germantown. We purchased a book of county maps of Tennessee from "County Maps," by C. J. Puetz of Lyndon, Wisconsin. This opened the door for bicycle travel all over Tennessee.

The first people we called when we decided to attempt to ride self-contained were Sid and Dot Cromwell of Murfreesboro. We had met them on our first BRAT ride and enjoyed them then and we have enjoyed their company on lots of rides since 1989. We began to ride from state park to state park. I would plot out our route and the four of us would meet in a state park and ride for the weekend.

Our first self-contained ride together was from Natchez Trace State Park to Mousetail Landing State Park. When we arrived at the park headquarters at Mousetail Landing, the two rangers on duty were impressed to see four bicyclists arrive to use the campground. The ranger announced that there was a steep climb to the campground. Sid and I just had to brag about all the mountains we had ridden. When we turned the corner to head for the campground, we faced the steepest climb I have ever completed without walking. Neither of us would give up and walk, so we stood in our lowest gear and zigged and zagged back and forth across the road until we reached the campground. From that day on, when anyone tells me there is a steep climb ahead, I just shake my head to agree with their observation, for they have seen the climb in most cases. I just want to be sure I am not locked into having to make the climb. I have learned to walk when it is necessary.

On other weekends we rode from Chickasaw State Park to Big Hill Pond State Park. We enjoyed riding alone and found great joy in riding in McNairy County. We know it was

Roscoe and Ann Phillips, riding on rural roads in Tennessee, loaded for traveling long distance.

the home of Buford Pusser, who had a rough reputation, but we found wonderful country roads with helpful people all along the routes. We would camp at Big Hill Pond State Park and ride several loops.

One weekend as we were riding from Big Hill Pond heading to Pickwick Landing State Park, a pickup truck passed us going in the opposite direction. The next thing we knew the truck was back and a lady was standing on the side of the road waving at us to stop. She introduced herself as Kay Horton and began to ask questions for an article she would write and publish in "The West Tennessee Guide," a newspaper published weekly in Ramer. This was not the first time we had been interviewed by a newspaper reporter. When a person sees a bicycle loaded with panniers, heading down a road or through town, it seems they just want to ask questions. "How far have you ridden?" "Where are you going?" Most of the response is, "I don't even drive my car that far." "How in the world can you stand that tiny little seat?" We get all sorts of questions.

1992 Calgary, Canada
The Perfect Bicycle Tour

With a short vacation on our hands, we searched for the perfect bicycle tour. We settled on Imagine Tours. This tour would take us from Memphis by plane to Calgary, Canada and then by bicycle from the airport to our hotel to meet the tour leaders and on to the Kananaskis Wilderness. From there we would ride over Hayward Pass and into Banff, with a day off to visit Lake Louise. The following day would take us to a Dude Ranch and then back to Calgary.

The second day out, we would have to stay in a Youth Hostel. This is the first time in our marriage we would not be allowed to sleep together. We attempted to set up our tent in an effort to avoid having to be in separate rooms, no way, as we were in bear country. This was our first youth hostel, never again, this we promised each other.

We rented a car and drove from Banff to Lake Louise. When we arrived at Lake Louise and walked into the hotel dining room over-looking the lake, we just had to eat next to the window. The maître d' made it very clear that it is very hot by the windows. Not to stop Ann, "We want to sit next to the window." No argument, we were seated next to the window and the perspiration began as soon as the maître d' had walked away from our table. The heat from the glass was like sitting under a magnifying glass and the longer we waited the hotter we became. This did not change Ann's mind, we remained by the window. We had the best view, and the hottest table in the restaurant. We were waited on and ate in a hurry in order to return to the outside world to cool off.

Since this was a tour, our tent and clothing were carried from one point to another. During the week it came time to camp in the wilderness, no showers, just a snow melt river to bathe in that evening. Some riders had brought sun-showers, these are water bags to hang in a tree and let the water, which had sat in the sun all day flow out for a warm shower. Not us, we bathed in the snow melt stream. It does not take long to bathe when the water is as cold as ice.

I explained to Ann how to wash in the river as I had hiked the PCT in 1985 and bathed in a lot of snow melt rivers and streams along the trail. "First you wash down as far as possible, then you wash up as far as possible, and then you wash "old possible." That is what my Aunt Amy Cash had taught me when I lived with her for a year as a child. So Ann and I washed "old possible" that evening in a snow melt stream in the Kananaskis Wilderness of Canada.

1994 Pocatello, Idaho to West Yellowstone, MT
"Let's Float the Snake at Dawn"

When we rode from Pocatello, Idaho to West Yellowstone, Montana, we arrived in Jackson Hole, Wyoming, on the Fourth of July, 1994. As we rode into town, a sign caught our eyes, "Free Breakfast for the First Float Trip on the Snake River". Wow! Free breakfast, say no more, we talked it up with the group of fellow bicyclists we had met and arranged for the float trip for the next morning. When we woke up that morning, guess what? There was frost on our tent, thick enough to write our names. Cold is cold and cold on the Snake is really cold. We ate our free breakfast and then loaded into the pontoon boats for the float down the Snake. Ann and I took the front tube seat along with a lady from the east and began to talk. The guide gave us instructions as to how to survive the rapids, but we heard only half of them. Something about reaching out and holding on to the rope in front of you. We were already cold when we arrived at the first rapids and when the guide said grab the ropes, we reached down between our legs and grabbed the rope. Wrong rope, not the one in front of us, this rope was all slack and we went over backwards into the bottom of the boat, which was filling up with the coldest water ever to fill a boat. There we were, all three of us rolling around in the bottom of the boat in ice water. From that point to the end of the float we understood why the first float trip received a free breakfast. Anyone in their correct mind would not float the Snake before the sun was shining into the Snake River Canyon. It was just too cold for humans.

All we could think of was, when will this end. When we arrived at the end of the float, our bus was waiting to take us back. Also, we had dry clothes on the bus, warm, dry clothes. The women took over the inside of the bus and that left the men outside in the open air to change clothes. Those of us brave enough to disrobe from the cold wet clothes did so. I was standing alongside the bus naked and attempting to redress when I looked up and one of the ladies was looking down at my naked body. As I looked, in shock that I had exposed myself, she said, "I can't see anything." I began to laugh and said I know; it is just too cold and held up my fore finger and thumb to indicate that the cold was about a half inch long. After that, the question was always, "Roscoe, how cold is it?" And I would hold up two fingers indicating about a half inch.

Traveling by Bicycle
Preparing for a Long-Distance trip:

Touring on a bicycle can take on many forms. There are state sponsored rides, touring companies, and just "do it your-self." We fit into the "do it yourself category." We have ridden on state sponsored rides and with touring companies, but the greatest feeling of freedom comes from just riding out our driveway and heading for Tampa, Florida or other destinations. Before anyone takes up bicycle touring there are several things to consider.

First, the proper bicycle for the type of touring you are planning to undertake. If you are going with a touring company, they will, in most cases, furnish the bicycle. If you are going it alone, paved roads offer you an opportunity to ride a touring bicycle with 26mm tires or less and a 120 plus PSI (pounds per square inch). With this setup, there is little road friction and the ability to cover longer distances is easier. We like the smooth easy ride of a paved road or better yet, a bicycle path. Ann and I ride Independent Fabrication Bicycles which we purchased through Outdoors, Inc. in 1999. One of the best tests in buying a bicycle! PICK IT UP! If it is so heavy you can hardly lift the bicycle it is too heavy for long distance. Also, remember you have to pick it up to place it on a bike rack.

Second, if you are going on a self-contained trip, then you need the best panniers for the ride. Our panniers are from Arkel out of Canada and they are considered the best of the best. Packing is a personal thing. We always carry a tent and sleeping bags, along with cooking gear. It is like having an insurance policy. If you do not use it, it is just luggage but if you hit a town where there are no rooms for rent. Guess what? You have a place to sleep.

Third, be sure you know something about bicycle repairs. Plan for the worst and wish for the best, is a good way to be prepared. When you are on your long-distance trips you will most likely have some type of problem. We carry two fold-up tires and five tubes to cover flats. We also carry spare chain parts and spokes. We do not carry a patch kit. It is easier to change one flat rather than to have the patch fail.

Fourth, plan your trip long in advance of the actual ride. We took mini-trips while preparing for the actual expeditions. We loaded our bicycles as if we were going the full distance. We went on over-night trips from our home to Meeman Shelby Forest State Park. The other mini trips were drives to either Chickasaw State Park or Big Hill Pond State Park and then we rode back to the other park. This made for great two-day rides. It also gave us a good look at the camping gear we were carrying. We corrected a lot of mistakes before we left for our trips.

Fifth, maps, good maps, really good maps, how can I say really good maps loud enough? In France, we used Michelin Maps and in the United States we acquired our maps from Adventure Cycling in Missoula, Montana. These are great resources for bicycle travel. You can acquire maps from the countries where you plan to ride. We used the internet to get maps of Finland and planned our trip from home before landing in Helsinki. Oh! Finland builds a bicycle road alongside all of their automobile roads. If you want to go to countries where bicycles have their own roads, The Netherlands, Belgium and Finland are three countries that we have toured on our own and enjoyed their bicycle roads. Other bicycle friendly countries to try are Ireland, France and China. They have fewer bicycle roads but the traffic is friendly. In Ireland, watch out for the cars with the left side mirror hanging by the cable. They are driven by the Americans! As it is very hard to judge how close the left side is to the hedge row, so off comes the mirror. We used "France by Bicycle", written by Karen & Terry Whitehill, to pick out several routes we rode in France and Belgium

I will quote from Cyd Mosteller, from the January 14, 2007, Commercial Appeal, "if you learn enough of the language to show good manners and greet everyone with a smile, you will feel at home in any country." Everyone you meet will return to you what you give to them. We have always been treated with kindness. We have been rescued from rain storms, and campgrounds from HELL. We have been invited to camp in people's yards or stay in their homes. We have met some of the greatest people while traveling on our bicycles.

I can say without hesitation, bicycling long distance has opened up a wonderful and exciting world to us. You can travel by bicycle, too. A quote from Joe Royer, of Outdoors. Inc., "If you are not in shape to ride long distance, you will be after the first month." So join the many people who love adventures, pick a place to travel by bicycle, research the area and go for a great adventure. It could be the best thing you ever do for yourself.

1995 Nova Scotia
The Winds Across the Straights of Bras d'Or

When we began to look for a place to ride self-contained, we thought of Nova Scotia as a safe place, few cars, friendly people and beautiful scenery. All of this came true when we rode across Nova Scotia.

This was our first self-contained long-distance vacation. We had decided to fly into Sydney, Nova Scotia, ride around the Cabot Trail, south across the Straights of Canzo, west to the Bay of Fundy, around to Yarmouth for the ferry back to the United States, landing in Bar Harbor, Maine.

We arrived late at the airport in Sydney and then had trouble putting our bicycles together. On the second bicycle I discovered that the bike shop in Memphis had packed the wheels for Ann's bicycle in the box with my bicycle and my wheels in the box with her bicycle. All of this was under the watchful eyes of the cab drivers waiting for the last plane to arrive in Sydney. After much confusion and losing my temper several times, I had reworked the brakes to fit the wrong wheels, unloaded and reworked the brakes for the correct wheels, and then reloaded about the time the sun was going

Nova Scotia
From Sydney to Yarmouth
August 11 to 25, 1995

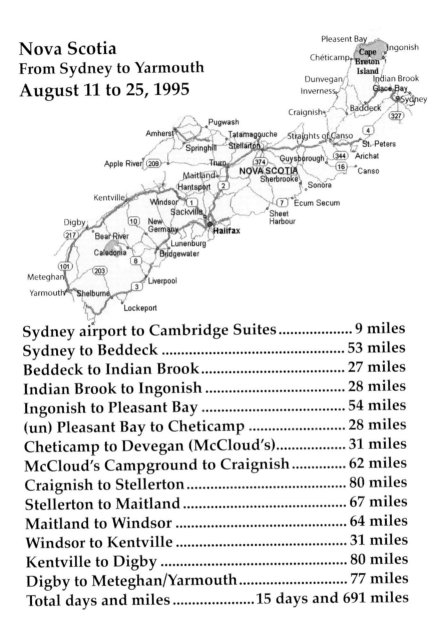

Sydney airport to Cambridge Suites	9 miles
Sydney to Beddeck	53 miles
Beddeck to Indian Brook	27 miles
Indian Brook to Ingonish	28 miles
Ingonish to Pleasant Bay	54 miles
(un) Pleasant Bay to Cheticamp	28 miles
Cheticamp to Devegan (McCloud's)	31 miles
McCloud's Campground to Craignish	62 miles
Craignish to Stellerton	80 miles
Stellerton to Maitland	67 miles
Maitland to Windsor	64 miles
Windsor to Kentville	31 miles
Kentville to Digby	80 miles
Digby to Meteghan/Yarmouth	77 miles
Total days and miles	15 days and 691 miles

down and darkness was coming to Sydney. We were still five miles from our hotel. Anywhere we have traveled by bicycle since, we have always drawn a crowd, but this was the first time. Ever since then, we expect the curious to gather around. The cab drivers adopted us, in a way, as they drove along behind us and directed us to our hotel. We arrived just short of darkness, and after the afternoon traffic had completed its run, we rolled off the road and into the lobby of our hotel.

The next morning, I looked out the window and the flags were standing straight out, flapping in the wind. Ann asked which direction we would have to ride and I laughed and stated in that direction and pointed in the direction the wind was coming from. True to bicycling, if you have a direction to ride and it is not your choice, it will always be into the wind. This was no different, we were heading out of Sydney and into the wind but luckily, we turned and picked up a tailwind as we headed to the Straights of Bras d'Or to cross Bras d'Or Lake. We approached the bridge over the Straights by way of a cut in a mountain and no wind, but as we rode out onto the bridge the cross wind hit us driving both bicycles across the bridge and into the guard rail, almost flipping us over the side and to a sudden death. There was much hanging onto the guard rail while holding onto the bicycles. We had trouble standing. We had trouble walking. We even had trouble just attempting to stand on the bridge and yet we had to cross the Straights of Bras d'Or in order to ride to Baddeck and our hotel for the night. I took my bicycle, holding it at a fifteen-degree angle I began to roll it along the railing as I crossed the bridge. I then returned to get Ann's bicycle and Ann and did much the same to cross. This would be the first of many bridges we have crossed with loaded bicycles and this bridge has set the stage for all crossings. When the wind blows and we approach a large bridge, the Straights of Bras d'Or is always mentioned.

We arrived in Baddeck that afternoon, and discovered that Scotland is the birth place of Alexander Graham Bell. He held a triple citizenship, British, Canadian and American. The Alexander Graham Bell National Historic Site is located in Baddeck, Cape Breton, Nova Scotia, overlooking the Bras d'Or Lake. The site includes the Alexander Graham Bell Museum, a unit of Parks Canada, which is the only museum in the world containing the actual artifacts and documents from Bell's years of experimental work in Baddeck. Besides the telephone, he experimented with building an anti-submarine hydrofoil which held the world's water speed record for several years. The museum covers a lot of his life and tells his story.

Our second day started out north toward the Cabot Trail to ride around the northern end of Nova Scotia. As we rode along, the traffic picked up, and when we arrived at St. Ann's we discovered the Gaelic Games at the Royal Cape Breton Gaelic College. We took the rest of the day off our bicycles to enjoy the Gaelic games, the many dance

groups, bands, and pipe and drum corps as they competed for trophies. When I asked a group of young ladies dressed in their Horn Pipe uniforms if I could photograph them, they got ready to perform the "Horn Pipe." They all lined up, placed their hands under their chins and posed for the photo. The photo is one I prize as it takes me back to St. Ann's each time I look at it.

When asked, "Where to next?" We would let them know we were riding the Cabot Trail around Cape Breton. Their reaction was "you'll never get up Old   Here   are   many stories of our long distance trips by bicycle and the wonderful people we met. These are stories of people, places and travels from our beginning as a couple, to retirement, and to the end of our ability to travel long distances by bicycle. It is sad and difficult to admit the fun of long distance travel by bicycle is over.

I hope these stories will bring a smile to your face, and encourage you to find your own adventures as you travel through life.

There were many training rides, in order to have the ability to ride our bicycles 60 to 80 miles per day. During our travels we rode 119 miles in one day. Read about that part of our travels in "The World Was Our Oyster, Until!" The "Until" is related to the events of 9/11, when the world changed from a trusting life style to one of mistrust. With the many changes, it made traveling by bicycle difficult and very expensive to fly with a bicycle.

We learned that "Old Smokey" would be the first of several mountains we would have to climb on our ride around Cape Breton. Mountains are always a concern when bicycling. After leaving St. Ann's in the rain, we found a B&B at Indian Brook, with a giant bathtub, and plenty of hot water for a good soaking. The next morning, we were warned again about

"Old Smokey." We rode north to connect with the Cabot Trail, and along the way we crossed the North River and began to climb. Ann was ahead of me, along the way I noticed a sign showing the down-hill curves and a warning of "Steep and Winding," I stopped, called Ann and asked "Are you at the top?" Meaning the top of "Old Smokey," and her reply was, "I suppose so, but this was nothing." We had climbed "Old Smokey," no pushing, no out of breath, and no problems with the climb. There were other warnings, such as "look out for North Mountain." We thought the rest of the ride would be a piece of cake.

We spent the night in Ingonish at the Island Inn and again we were warned about North Mountain. We smiled knowing we had climbed "Old Smokey" and North Mountain could not be harder. Well, we found out the mountains around the Cabot Trail do get harder, steeper, and longer. On the third night along the Cabot Trail, we planned to stay at the Salty Mariner in Pleasant Bay. The night before in Pleasant Bay, there had been a group of young bicyclists at the Salty Mariner. We passed them on their way around the Cabot Trail going in the opposite direction of our trip. They did not appear to be friendly, so we rode on toward Pleasant Bay. When we arrived at the Salty Mariner, the owner was not happy to see more bicyclists, as the group the night before had been very loud and destructive. When she saw us arriving and I asked where to put our bicycles, she pointed across the lawn, and said "they are not to be any closer than that if you want to stay here." Well, we judged Pleasant Bay as the only Unpleasant Bay we found in Nova Scotia.

From Unpleasant Bay we rode to Cheticamp for the night and completed the ride around the Cabot Trail. On our last day, we had more of a problem on the descent than any climb, as it was steeper than the other side of the mountains along the Cabot Trail. From Mackenzies Point to Cheticamp, we rode our brakes and prayed they would hold on the ride down.

We found a place to stay and went out for lunch. The restaurant we chose was full, with a long wait time. I noticed they were seating tables of four before they were taking tables for two, so being brave I asked the couple in front of us if they wanted to share a table, "No thanks" was the reply. But the couple behind us spoke up and said "we'll share a table," we changed from a table for two to a table for four. We were seated long before the couple who had refused to join us. We introduced ourselves and found we had joined up with a couple with the last name of "McFarlan," Ann's maiden name. Of course, Ann let them know she was a McFarlan and immediately she was told "you look just like his grandmother." By the time we had finished lunch, Ann was kin to the McFarlans from Nova Scotia. We learned of the McFarlan Woods, and other exciting McFarlan locations. The next day we rode to Dunvegan and stayed at McCloud's Campground for the night.

Gillis McCloud's Campground
and
French Press Coffee

McCloud's Beach and Campsite is located on the western side of Cape Breton Island, twelve kilometers north of the village of Inverness. When we arrived just, short of dark and set up our tent, we were welcomed to the campground by Mr. McCloud himself. We also noticed a flyer on the wall, "Pizza delivered to the campground, minimum order, $16.00." So, how much would we spend on a cab to and from Inverness, and for dinner in town? What we cannot eat we would share with the other campers, a no brainer, and it would save money and time. When we called the pizza place, they declined our order and that left us with only one choice, the cab to and from town to eat dinner. We searched through the many options in the local phone book for places to eat and made a choice, called the cab and informed the cab driver where we wanted to go eat. "No! You do not want to eat there, I know a better restaurant with great food." Later, we discovered the cab driver and the restaurant owner were kin to each other. We had dinner and returned to the campground to sleep. The next morning, we packed for an early start. We rode to the camp store, looking for coffee, no coffee! "What?" No coffee!" Then Ann asked Mr. McCloud if he was sending us off for twelve kilometers without coffee, he said "Wait a minute, little lady." He picked up the phone, called the big house, and when his son Gillis answered the phone he said, "Gillis, I am sending a Yank couple up to the house, give them some coffee and send them on their way." When we arrived at the house, Gillis was boiling water. This was the first time we ever had French Press Coffee. We learned one thing in Nova Scotia, they take care of their own. If you need a cafe, a B&B, or cab service, they are very likely to send you to a service owned by a relative.

 I bragged on the friendly drivers and how much room they gave us when passing and Gillis said, "that's understandable, cows, little old ladies, and bicyclists are all unpredictable. You give all of them a wide birth."

Oh!
Never Float the Bay of Fundy
We Did it For You.

We completed our ride around Cape Breton by crossing the Straights of Canso after a night at the Craft-Works B&B in Creignish. It had been a school and the lady owner had converted it into a B&B. We stopped and asked about dinner close by and she said we could take her truck if we stayed the night and we could drive into Aulds Cove for dinner. I asked if she was concerned that we would take her truck and run, she said, "I'm not worried, I have your bicycles".

From the Straights of Canso, we rode southwest along the Bay of Fundy to Stellarton and then into Maitland with reservations at the Foley House Inn. We also had a reservation to ride up the tidal bore in Cobequid Bay. This is the highest tidal bore in Nova Scotia, as I stated in the title of this segment, we did it for you, so you do not have to float the tidal surge in Cobequid Bay. There is a bridge over the bay about thirty minutes into the ride, go there and watch the people who are riding the tidal bore. In the end, you will thank me for saving you from this experience.

Now to explain this ride up the tidal bore. It was our sixth anniversary and also the anniversary of another couple in the rubber raft. When we arrived at the point of departure, the rubber raft was sitting on the bottom of Cobequid Bay in the mud about 300 yards out in the middle of the Bay. We waded in the mud to the raft, and now we have the muddiest running shoes we have ever had. Oh! I forgot to mention, the shoes were "brand-new" and the only shoes we had other than the bicycle snap-on shoes for the pedals. The raft was full of passengers waiting for the tidal surge to arrive and it did little by little, starting with the gurgling sound of water arriving. Soon the gurgle turned into a roar and we were lifted up and out of the mud to ride the tidal bore up Cobequid Bay and under the bridge covered with people waving us on our way.

Since this was a late afternoon start, it began to get dark, and cold. We were already muddy, now, we were wet and muddy, and cold, really cold, everyone was wondering when this would be over, when suddenly out came sandwiches and orange drinks. That is correct, orange drinks. This is our anniversary and we are having orange drinks in a rubber raft, cold, muddy, wet, and wishing we could end this ride. I asked the guide how we would know when we had arrived at the finish, he stated they would flash him with a flash-light. It was now so dark one could hardly see one's hand in front of one's face. Suddenly, a light, a cheer from the raft, and a rope was tossed to us to help in stopping this raft as it was propelled up the Cobequid Bay by the tidal surge. When we finally tied up to the shore, our guide said to be careful ascending the bank as it was slippery. Slippery was not something we wanted to hear, and sure enough Ann fell flat on her back and slid down the bank toward the raft. I was holding the rope, collected Ann and now we are a wet, cold mud ball. We loaded on the bus for the return trip to Maitland.

The owner of the Foley House Inn knew the returning visitors would be wet, cold, muddy, and tired, so he was sitting on the porch of the Foley House Inn, and said, "there is a water hose to your right, take off your shoes and leave them in the yard, wash your feet before coming onto the porch." We did. So, if you are ever in Maitland and tempted to ride the tidal bore in Cobequid Bay, DON'T. It is cold, muddy, long, and believe me the orange soda is not worth the experience.

From Maitland to Windsor and on to Kentville!

The following day we attempted to wash our shoes, clean the mud off our clothes and get ready to ride to Windsor. Then to the port of Kentville. Kentville is where the English had expelled the French Acadians known as Cajuns in the United States. So all the good cooking came to the States and left Kentville without a cook but they have beer! Yes! Beer and very good beer, as we attempted to revive ourselves and get back to some kind of normality. We rode our bicycles from the Wandlynn Motel to a local tavern to comfort ourselves over the loss of our shoes. We looked for a local restaurant for dinner and found a tavern. Great idea, it worked out to be one of the better ideas we had in Nova Scotia, when it comes to eating. I asked if they had any dark beer, yes! We brew all our beers and if you would like a sampler, I will get you one. Thinking it would be just a shot of beer as she stated they had five (5) different beers. Wrong they were the "old nickel beer glasses" and five of them was more beer than Ann normally drinks as she is a one beer person. After we finished the samples, we found out they were free, so to show them our appreciation, we ordered two beers. They were in much larger glasses. By the time we had finished dinner and five small glasses and one large glass of beer, we wondered if we should not walk back to the motel. We rode!

From Kentville to Digby!

In Nova Scotia there was a reservation service called "Check-in Nova Scotia." It was operated by the Nova Scotia tourist service. We discovered it when we arrived and each day we would check with them to find a place to stay the next day. We were heading to Digby and looking forward to scallops. Digby Scallops are famous. So, when I called the reservation service the young lady said, "I was so hoping you would go to Digby, there is a B&B by the name of Ocean Hillside B&B." "Can you climb up a steep hill?" "Yes!" "We can get to it even if we have to push." We stayed at the Ocean Hillside B&B in Digby. The owner was a retired chef from the Hilton Hotels and that evening they drove us into the harbor for scallops. The next morning the "Tall Ships" had come into Digby Harbor. They were standing tall in the rising sun, as we sat in front of a picture window overlooking the harbor, and ate the best breakfast served in Nova Scotia at any B&B.

From Digby to Yarmouth
Catching the Blue Nose!

After fifteen (15) days and 691 miles on the road we arrived in Yarmouth to catch the ferry back to Bar Harbor, Maine to end our ride around Nova Scotia and our first fully loaded bicycle ride. When we stopped at the ticket booth to purchase our tickets to Bar Harbor, the lady in the booth began to shout "I don't believe it," " I don't believe it." "I asked what she did not believe," "Even your shoes match." We had not planned our dress code or even thought about it other than we wear the same bicycle jerseys when we ride, but our shoes, we had never thought about the shoes. This trip set up the many more rides we did in the years ahead and gave us a new insight into traveling by bicycle.

1996 Sierra to the Sea Across California

Sierra to the Sea is a scenic and challenging eight-day bicycle and camping tour. The ride begins at Columbia in the gold fields of California, crosses the Sierra Nevada Mountain range, then down to Folsom and into Sacramento, through Davis to Calistoga, Napa Valley, the Russian River Valley, and on to the Pacific Coast at Duncans Mills. The tour finishes with a ride across the Golden Gate Bridge and a picnic in Golden Gate Park. The Almaden Cycle Touring Club takes two busloads of bicyclists across the state to Columbia, along with their gear. At the end of the tour everyone bicycles over the Golden Gate Bridge. This is a camping tour, no hotels, but each night we were served dinner on China plates, cloth napkins, and proper cutlery. Everyone was encouraged to bring their own wine.

Along the way we saw Folsom prison, and visited the state capitol in Sacramento. When we arrived in the wine valleys, we were encouraged to purchase a bottle for a wine tasting at Duncans Mills. They carried the bottles for each rider. We rode through Davis and visited the UC Davis campus but the most fun came when we reached Calistoga.

If you have never had a mud bath, Calistoga is the place for your first experience. Calistoga Spa Hot Springs is a geothermal mineral water resort located in the upper Napa Valley town of Calistoga. It was our first experience but not the last, as we did it a second time in Haapsalu Estonia. Each time was a wonderful, refreshing experience. We highly recommend taking a mud bath when offered.

When we left Davis, we teamed up with a couple from San Jose. They suggested we buy a picnic lunch and we did. They were riding a tandem. This was during the time of the Gray Poupon commercials with a limo always asking "Do you have any Gray Poupon?" As we were riding along, we met a limo. It turned around and returned alongside the tandem bicycle. The back window was lowered and a hand came out and asked, "Do you have any Gray Poupon?" And the lady on the tandem reached back into the picnic basket and pulled out the Gray Poupon and said, "But of course." Everyone in the limo roared and we laughed as much as they did. We did have Gray Poupon at the picnic and created a lasting friendship.

Upon arriving in Duncans Mills, the tour guides had set up a table and opened all the bottles of wine they had carried across California. When you are riding with a crowd in their twenties and they think they should have a sample of each bottle, well the camp was full of drunks and sick riders. The tour group gave us a ride to dinner on the busses that evening. One of the riders named Bob, had found "Bob's Very Good Red Table Wine" and we sampled his find and decided it was not any better than "Bob's Very Good White Table Wine" which his riding companion had purchased.

From Duncans Mills, we rode across the Golden Gate Bridge. I had lived in San Francisco in 1956 to 1958 and never found it warm enough to enjoy walking across the Bridge, but on this day it was perfect. The weather was warm and the fog was gone. Everyone was treated to a picnic in Golden Gate Park. We said our goodbyes to all the new friends except Bob and Nancy. They took us to their home. We toured the Rodin Garden at Stanford University before returning home.

The tour route is approximately 420 miles long and averages 60 miles per day. It is challenging and designed for experienced riders. Sierra to the Sea is organized by the Almaden Cycle Touring Club of San Jose.

Utah in 1996 (the second ride of 1996)
"There is Fat Tire Beer in Cheyenne, Wyoming"

In 1996, Ann and I decided to drive to Utah and join up with a group of bicyclists in St. George's and ride to Logan to celebrate the centennial of Utah. The same year Tennessee was celebrating its bicentennial. First, we decided to drive to Logan and catch the bus from Logan to St.. George and ride back to our car and then drive back home.

On our way we stopped in Cheyenne, Wyoming for an over-night stop before continuing on to Logan. We thought it would be great to have a real Wyoming steak. We asked the lady at the motel where to find the best steaks in Cheyenne? Her reply was, about twenty miles south into Colorado. We were not driving to Colorado for a steak when we were in the steak capitol of America, Cheyenne, Wyoming. So, we decided to drive into downtown and just have a look around. We began by walking around town, looking for a restaurant, no luck, we didn't know where to look. We spotted a pub and decided, pub food was good in Nova Scotia so why not try it in Cheyenne. We stuck our heads into the pub but it was not anything like the pubs we had found to eat in, in Nova Scotia. As we were retreating, the lady behind the bar said, "come on in," "no thanks, we are looking for a steak." "Best steak in Wyoming, right down stairs in the Furnace Room." "Can we get there through here?" "Sure can." We did, we walked over to a stairway leading down to the basement and found our way to the Furnace Room. If you are ever in

Cheyenne be sure to eat in the Furnace Room, best steak you will find anywhere. The service was great and the waitress asked us if we cared for a drink, sure, do you have a wine list. We enjoy merlot. Then it dawned on me a lot of places have a mini-brewery, "Is there a mini-brewery here in town?" "No!" "But we have Fat Tire Beer." Well, since we ride bicycles, we ordered Fat Tire Beer. The waitress brought only one bottle. It stood over a foot tall and held twenty-two ounces of beer. Ann and I split the beer.

We left the next morning for Logan and laughed about the size of the bottle used by Fat Tire Beer. Occasionally we would think of Marty and Susan, Ann's daughter and son-in-law, and laugh about taking them several bottles of Fat Tire Beer, just because of the size of the bottle and of course the great taste of Fat Tire Beer. I know it reads as though I am trying to impress the owners or the brew-master at Fat Tire Beer. Just in case they read this part of my book and decide, they should send Roscoe and Ann a few bottles for mentioning their beer, I want them to know we did enjoy the brew as well as the great packaging, a twenty-two-ounce bottle.

I know you are probably wondering what this has to do with riding our bicycles across Utah. Well, we also had to return to Cheyenne. Now here is where the fun began. Ann had two first cousins in the whole world. One lived in New York in 1996 but Norman Roome passed away in 2000, and the other lived in Novato, California, north of San Francisco. This is Peter Roome. When we arrived in Cheyenne it was 10 a.m. and the Furnace Room was closed, also the pub upstairs. We were in luck; a cleaning crew was leaving the building and I asked where we could purchase Fat Tire Beer at this time of the morning. The young man replied, well about a mile or so out that street you'll come to DT's, you can't miss it, it has a big pink elephant in front of the place. Now this is ten o'clock in the morning and the place is full of people drinking on a Monday morning. Folks, this just doesn't happen where I grew up, people work on Mondays and drink from Friday night until Sunday morning and those who can, go to church, those who can't, work on getting over their hangover.

We had entered through the bar and headed for the liquor store in front of the building, I thought I heard someone say, "Ann." Then as I rounded a stack of boxes, Peter Roome, said, "Roscoe, what are you doing in Cheyenne, Wyoming?" "I'm buying Fat Tire Beer. What are you doing in Cheyenne Wyoming, Peter Roome?" "I'm buying Fat Tire Beer." What a great surprise to have a wonderful visit with a cousin under such amazing circumstances. Come to find out, he and his wife come to Cheyenne each year to play golf with friends. When we called Ann's daughter in Memphis we asked, "Guess who we ran into in Cheyenne in a liquor store?" "Peter Roome, why?" "Who else would you run into in a liquor store in Cheyenne?"

Now back to our ride across Utah, we met a lot of wonderful people and enjoyed their state in the process. As the ride progressed, we camped, stayed in state parks, national parks, amusement parks, camped on school grounds and in the gyms and one night in a Presbyterian Prep School, named the Wasatch Academy. Now here is where our fun began. Ann was having trouble with her bicycle and it was repaired by Bingham Cyclery. He would not accept payment for the work and we had seen him and his crew enjoying a glass of wine the night before. So, we decided to purchase a bottle of wine for him and present it to him and his crew at the end of the day. Have you ever attempted to purchase wine in Utah? It is not the easiest state in the US to purchase wine or liquor. They have state liquor stores and one cannot just walk up to a wine rack, read the labels and decide which wine to purchase. Also, they have a poor selection out in rural Utah. We found a state liquor store about noon and after much discussion with the lady in charge, we decided to purchase two bottles of wine, one for Bingham Cyclery and one for ourselves.

One thing I can say about the worker at the liquor store, she had the ability to see into the future. She said "Let me put them in two plastic bags just in case they are broken, they will not get all over everything." Now when the liquor lady says that, please take heed for that will give you reason to be concerned. Also, Wasatch Academy is Presbyterian and being a deacon in the Presbyterian Church. I knew better than to bring wine onto the church grounds. We have to drink grape juice on communion Sunday. The people in charge of the ride had also announced that morning not to bring liquor onto the academy grounds. With all this attention to detail, one would think a lot of care would be taken to sneak a couple bottles of wine onto the grounds and into our room. First, I delivered the bottle to Bingham and his crew and received a wonderful thank you for the wine. Second, I returned to our room and there on the floor lay my bicycle with a broken bottle of wine inside a plastic bag, just as the liquor lady had foreseen. The wine was inside the bag and the bag was full of glass. There was not any way to strain the wine. So, I had the honor of removing the bag of wine from the room, through the lobby of the dorm, and into a waste basket outside of the building. As I attempted to pass unnoticed through the lobby, I heard shouts from the crowd of fellow bicyclists, "You can't have liquor in the dorm." Did you ever want to kill the bearer of bad news? I felt like killing all of them. Then the academy would never know who broke the bottle of wine in the dorm, and I would never have to admit that it was I.

On our third day of the ride Ann and I passed a farm with a pen of goats near the road. When we stopped to look at the goats a young man about six or seven years of age came out to explain how the goats were separated. After much discussion he decided we should see all of his farm animals. He led the way around the barn to a pen where there were several young goats. He climbed into the pen and immediately they began to jump up on him, not in standing up but on his back as he would bend over to lift one for us to admire. This went on for several minutes and Ann and I thought he was going to be hurt by the pounding he was receiving from the number of goats jumping up on him. Before long he became a little tired of the events and decided to show us his sheep, hogs, cows, horses and then to explain to us which animals were to be eaten, which ones they would sell and which ones they would keep for use on their farm.

We spent about thirty minutes with him before his mother stuck her head out the back door to find out how he was and if all was well. Now in a large city, I feel a parent would have been out in a hurry to find out who these strangers are walking around their yard. This is rural Utah and Mormon country, both spell trust in people. The people of Utah went all out to make sure we enjoyed our bicycle ride across their state and the celebration of statehood for 100 years.

1997 Quebec City to Ottawa

We rode from Quebec City to Ottawa along the St. Lawrence Seaway and up the Ottawa River to Ottawa, a distance of 560 miles in seventeen days, self-contained. The mileage includes total miles in the cities and side trips such as our side trip to Sainte Anne de Beaupre from Quebec City. This was a great seventeen-day self-contained trip through the French speaking part of Canada, but what did I do but choose the wrong direction. East to West is not the direction to travel on a bicycle in Canada. Think of the direction of the wind and you will understand the problem of riding to the west. One day we met a couple on fat-tired bikes averaging 24 mph to our 8 mph on 24 mm tires, not good when you are the one who picked out the direction to ride. The other bicyclists with you can always say "I told you so, or if you had asked me."

From the airport in Quebec City we rode into the part of Quebec City know as Old Town where we had reserved a B&B. As we rode along, we encountered a dapper gentleman on a bicycle riding up beside us who said, "Welcome to Quebec City." "Let me show you my beautiful city." So, we began a journey through Quebec City with a guide on a bicycle. Soon though he turned into a one-way street going the wrong way, with Ann in tow. I stopped, watched, and waited for the two to turn around and return with cars pushing them in the correct direction, not to be! They disappeared around a corner and out of sight. I began to ride in the direction I had last seen them heading and after a street or two, I saw them sitting on a bench overlooking the St. Lawrence River. When I stopped and sat down, the conversation was about where we would go from Quebec City. I explained that we planned to ride to Sainte Anne de Beaupre Basilica. "He asked?" "Will you pray when you go to Sainte Anne de Beaupre?" "Yes!" "Do you plan to visit Cathedral-Basilica of Notre-Dame here in Quebec City?" "Yes" "Will you pray?" "Well yes." "Then where will you go from Quebec City?" "We plan to visit Montreal, and the Notre-Dame Basilica of Montréal." "Will you pray?" "Oh I suppose so." "Then where?" "We plan to ride to Oka." "Oka!" "Will you pray when you get to Oka?" "No, we plan to buy cheese." "By the way what do you do for a living?" "I'm a priest. I am home on leave from Africa." "And where will you go from Oka?" I explained that we would ride to Ottawa before returning home. He gave us a history lesson about Quebec City as we sat on the overlook above the Saint Lawrence River.

We did have a wonderful ride along the Saint Lawrence River. First, we rode east to Sainte Anne de Beaupre and then back through Quebec City. Along our route from Sainte Anne de Beaupre, we decided to cross over to Ill de Orleans for a ride around the island. This was a beautiful day with light wind and plenty of sunshine and a great island to bicycle around. The island is dotted with Irish potato fields and raspberry patches. We found a small village and purchased a bag of local dark chocolate candy for a snack. This would pay big later in the ride when the rain came during a stop to purchase raspberries. The small roadside stand was run by a couple in their sixties, so we identified with them in age. They told us the rain was coming and to join them on their porch to get out of the rain. This we did, when the rain hit, we began to eat our candy and berries. We offered the candy to them, and they joined us and furnished even more raspberries. So, we had increased our raspberries by extending a friendly offer of chocolate candy.

By the time the rain was over and we returned to the bridge to cross over to the mainland, the wind had returned in earnest. We took one look at the bridge and considered the wind; we did not want to repeat our experience of crossing the Straights of Bras d'Or on the Cabot Trail in Nova Scotia. We stopped in a gas station near the foot of the bridge and discussed our options. Soon a tow truck arrived for a cup of coffee. We asked what he would charge to drive us over the bridge. He quoted ten dollars. We jumped at the bargain, rather than taking a chance of being blown off the bridge. He was quite funny about the tow job as it was his first ever bicycle tow job. He hooked up his crane and lifted our loaded bicycles, and said, "This is part of the fare." I was pleased not to have to unload or lift a seventy-pound bicycle up to the bed of the truck. After the tow over the bridge he found a safe spot to drop us off and we were again on our way back to Quebec City heading west.

Trois-Rivières

"the Quebecois-type Ladies" B&B

We rode along the St. Lawrence River to another very long and very high bridge over the St. Lawrence, into Trois-Rivières. When we found a tourist information center, we stopped in to ask about B&B's along our route west on the south side of the St. Lawrence. The young man said he knew of one if we did not mind staying with a couple of "Quebecois-type ladies." We said we did not and he directed us to Gîte L'Aubergelle along the St. Lawrence. We were welcomed by two ladies with open arms and a warm drink. That evening we were treated to a dinner, wine included and then a great night's sleep. The breakfast was delicious and we were given two tee shirts to remember them by. Gîte L'Aubergelle was located in Nicolet, Quebec on the Nicolet River. This was a few miles south of the St. Lawrence but the detour was well worth the side trip to the Gîte L'Aubergelle.

When we left their Gite, we traveled on west along the St. Lawrence river with a side trip up the Richelieu River. Our next stop along the ride came in the form of a fast ride just ahead of a rain and a B&B overlooking the Richelieu River. As we crossed the Richelieu, we found a pay phone and had just enough change to make a call to the number listed for a B&B. We asked if there was a room, learned there was, and rode hard to beat the rain.

The owner's son met us as we rode into the yard and signaled for us to place our bicycles under the back of the house out of the rain. He then said he had to go but his father was on the way and would let us in the house. The son left and shortly afterward the father arrived, and said "I'm Mr. Poisson, in the States I would be Mr. Fisher, as they changed Poisson to Fisher as they processed them into the USA." I then introduced Ann and myself to him and he almost ran us through the house showing us our side of the house, that we could make ourselves at home as he had to run. He said he was attending a garden party and must return. I then asked where we could eat dinner and he said, "There are two restaurants." "Oh!" "Just go to the first one on the left."

Later that day when it came time for dinner, Ann and I dressed in our rain suits and walked to the first restaurant on the left. As we entered, the maître d' looked surprised and said, "Oh!" "You are the guests of Mr. Poisson! He stopped by and made a reservation for you next to the window." Here is a man who was in a rush to return to a garden party, but he took time to reserve a table for us overlooking the Richelieu. Nice surprises have come our way every time we travel by bicycle. We had breakfast with Mr. and Mrs. Poisson the next morning overlooking the Richelieu, as the sun rose, we had a clear day to continue on toward Montreal.

Crossing into Montreal
A Bicycle Ferry
Across the Saint Lawrence River

After leaving the Richelieu River, we headed north to Montreal. As with any river, we worried about the type of crossing. When we approached Montreal, we were welcomed with a bicycle path along the Saint Lawrence River. We began to talk to other bicyclists as we were loaded and were asked the usual questions. How far have you come? Where are you from? And the questions go on and on. We asked them also: How do we cross the Saint Lawrence River? The answer was simple, catch the "Bicycle Ferry." Yes! There is a bicycle ferry. It was a great relief to know all we had to do was pay our fare, load the bicycles into the bike rack and ride across the river. Montreal has over 200 km's of designated bicycle lanes and also stand-alone bike paths. We spent a couple of days in Montreal before heading for Oka.

Let's go to Oka and Smell the Cheese!

Our next stop was in Oka, a small town located on the Ottawa River. We wanted to visit the Abbey of Notre-Dame du Lac, known as the Oka Abbey. It was a Trappist Cistercian monastery. The main monastery building was made of grey stone; it had a dozen outbuildings, all of which are situated on a 270-hectare property. They produce the Oka Cheese, with its distinctive flavor and aroma. Once you smell Oka Cheese you will always recognize that cheese. We bought cheese, bread and a bottle of wine and rode off looking for a place along the Ottawa River to picnic.

As we began our picnic, we heard a noise we recognized, that of fast-moving bicycles. It was the annual ride from Ottawa to Quebec City. As they passed we saluted them with a glass of wine and the loaf of bread and they shouted "Bon voyage," a French phrase used by the English, usually translated as, "have a nice trip."

From Oka to Ottawa
The end of a great ride!

Ottawa was a welcome sight as the ride into the wind was over, but the beauty of the trip continued. We checked into a B&B in Ottawa along the Rideau Canal. The Rideau Canal, also known unofficially as the Rideau Waterway, connects Canada's capital city of Ottawa, Ontario, to Lake Ontario and the Saint Lawrence River at Kingston, Ontario. In the winter it is referred to as the Rideau Skate-way as it freezes over and the Canadians use it as a skating rink. While we were in Ottawa, we visited the Capital of Canada and the National Gallery of Canada which is home to more than 40,000 works of art.

After a few days in Ottawa it was time to catch a plane for home, and of course, to figure out how to get to the airport. This was a Sunday flight home and when we talked to the B&B owner about how to get to the airport, he did not understand the problem. His question was "what is the problem?" How to get two bicycles and bags to the airport, I thought we would need a cab or truck. Then we learned the greatest news of all about riding a bicycle in Ottawa on Sunday mornings. From 7:00 a.m. until 1:00 p.m., all of the parkways in Ottawa are closed to automobile traffic and only open to bicyclists, walkers, joggers, runners, skate-boarders, roller-bladders and any other mechanical forms of travel, but no motorized vehicles. After seventeen days of travel from Quebec City to Ottawa, we were not ready to come home, but life requires that a person return to earn money for the next trip.

Vancouver to the Pacific Rim
Around the Sunshine Coast

In July of 1998, we flew out to Vancouver to meet Clay and Jan Simon for a two-week vacation. They were traveling in a motor camper and we were on our bicycles. When we camped at the same campground, they carried our panniers, we rode all day and met up in the evenings for a happy hour. That was how we spent our vacation in 1998.

When we arrived in Vancouver, our bicycles were delivered through a separate baggage door onto the floor of the luggage room. Everyone else had picked up their luggage and left the airport before the bicycles and boxes with the panniers came through the oversize luggage doors. We began to unpack and I asked the person in the luggage room if there was a place to discard the boxes. He said to leave them where you are, load your bicycles and ride out of the airport. This was a very large room with plenty of space to ride with no one else in the room. We did as he suggested. We rode across the luggage room toward the lobby. The automatic exit door opened for us and standing on the other side was a terminal full of people waiting for the next passengers to arrive. When they saw us a loud gasp came from the crowd, then laughter and then they broke out into a loud applause. We had arrived and with great fanfare! From the airport, we rode on bike paths and designated streets into downtown Vancouver.

This vacation was from July 30, to August 16, 1998. We arrived on a Thursday and our reservations were at the Douglas Guest House. The next day we took a bus tour of the city and found out there would be a fireworks display on Saturday night. We stayed at the B&B for three nights before departing for the bicycle ride on Sunday morning.

On Saturday evening we caught a very over-crowded bus into the city to see the fireworks from Jericho Beach. Out in the bay was a large barge loaded with fireworks. This was part of the International Fireworks Contest. This weekend just so happened to be the fireworks for the country of Spain. People were spread out everywhere and we became people watchers as the least dressed arrived, along with the overdressed and one Boa Constrictor! A small contingent of young men with a very large snake were making the rounds and placing the snake over people's shoulders for those who wanted a photo with the snake. We had all kinds of thoughts as the snake was passed around and just how it would react when the fireworks started. We soon lost sight of the snake and began to watch as one of the greatest fireworks displays began.

After the fireworks, we learned what it was like to move through the city with four-hundred thousand (400,000) people. It was a mob, but that night everyone came away from the fireworks in a great mood. We walked and walked and walked almost all the way back to the B&B before we were able to catch a bus. We did not see the snake after the show began. We hadn't planned this part of the vacation as we didn't know about the International Fireworks Competition, but were lucky we arrived on the best weekend to be in Vancouver, BC.

On Sunday morning we rode south to catch the ferry from Tsawwassen to Nanaimo on Vancouver Island. In order to get to the Tsawwassen ferry terminal one had to go through the George Massey Tunnel. In a car, there would be no problem, but on a bicycle, there was a problem. How do you ride through a tunnel with cars? This is the question we asked ourselves as we approached the tunnel. Just before our entrance into the tunnel, there was a sign with an arrow pointing to the right, bicycles exit here. Now what do we do? Lo and behold, sitting in front of us was a Canadian Highway Van, markings and all with a trailer hooked on the back, with some bicycles on the trailer for the ride through the George Massey Tunnel and on to Tsawwassen. A very tall Indian Sikh, was waiting for bicyclists to give them a ride through the tunnel. This service was provided by the Canadian government, free for anyone going through the tunnel on foot or bicycle. When we arrived on the south end of the tunnel, he pulled into a parking lot, unloaded the bicycles and sent us on our way. The other bicyclists were out for a Sunday ride and escorted us into the ferry terminal. It was another wonderful start for a great bicycle trip through British Columbia, Canada.

We landed in Nanaimo about noon and had a very hilly ride to the Big Tent RV Park near Parksville, where Clay and Jan Simon were waiting for our arrival. They presented Ann with a glass of wine and me with a beer and welcomed us to the Pacific Rim. The next day, Clay and Jan carried our panniers and we rode without any load out to the Pacific Rim to Sproat Lake for the night. The next day we rode to Ucluelet and camped at the Pacific Rim National Park.

This would be a two-night stay as we decided to kayak with a park leader. This was our first attempt at kayaking. He explained how to sit on the side of the pier and slide into the kayak and how to paddle. Soon we were off and of course we quickly fell behind the other kayaks. They just kept going and going. We suddenly looked up and saw that we were in the path of seaplanes. We were in the landing strip for the sightseeing seaplanes. We attempted to speed up but they just kept coming. As we exited the sea strip, they passed by without hitting any of the kayaks coming across the strip. We were not the slowest but we were not anywhere close to the front. After our stay at Ucluelet, Clay and Jan said their good-byes and we were off on our own.

We had discovered a foot-ferry from Ucluelet to Port Alberni. In order to catch the ferry at Ucluelet for Port Alberni, we had to be at the ferry dock at 1:30 p.m. to catch the ferry at 2:00 p.m. to arrive in Port Alberni at 7 p.m. to stay overnight in Port Alberni. We were staying at the Alberni Inn.

From Port Alberni we rode to Denman Island with plans to camp at Fillongley Provincial Park. This is a walk-in camp site. Since saying our good-byes to Clay and Jan and being on our own, we could ride at our own leisure. We were planning to ride around the Sunshine Loop and back to Nanaimo before heading to Victoria and then over to Anacortes, Washington.

Along the way we had reservations at Port Gibson at the Bonniebrook Lodge. As we approached the lodge, a surprise was waiting for us, Clay and Jan Simon. The next day we did another kayak trip around the islands. When Ann and I sat on the side of the dock to slide into the kayak, the lady in charge looked at us and asked. "What are you doing?" "Stand up and step into the kayak, this is a sea kayak and if it tips over, I'll give you the kayak." We attempted to explain that the leader of the kayak trips out at the Pacific Rim had us sit and slide into the kayak. This was different. After a day on the water we headed to Victoria and a trip to Butchart Gardens.

As we rode to the ferry to start our trip to Anacortes, we encountered a bicyclist on an eight-hundred-mile trip. Ann began to quiz him on how he planned the trip and informed him we wanted to ride across the USA. He asked, "When do you want to do this ride?" When Ann told him we wanted to do it next year, he said. "Here is how you do it. When you get home from this ride you tell everyone that you are going to ride across the USA next year, and then you will have to." So we did and the planning began.

On Ann's birthday we camped on Orcas Island at Moran State Park and climbed to the top of the island to view as far as we could see across Puget Sound. The next day we rode the ferry into Anacortes and visited Virginia and Jack Haywood, with a promise that when we returned to ride across the USA we would again visit. We did!

Seattle to Bar Harbor
Across the USA in Three Months

When we returned to Germantown, we began to tell everyone that we were going to ride our bicycles across the USA and then we had to, just as the young man had stated. I told my boss, that I would retire on March 20, 1999 and he explained that I could retire earlier and he would help with my health insurance, and other expenses. So, I did! As I was leaving the shop, one of the younger workers said, "Roscoe, did they let you go?" I said "They sure did." And walked out to retire early in 1999.

Stop and think for a moment. It is 4,396 miles from Seattle, Washington to Bar Harbor, Maine by bicycle. Now think of this, it is 2,225 miles from Seattle, Washington to Bemidji, Minnesota and you are just a little over half way to Bar Harbor, Maine. You have just crossed the Mississippi River at Lake Itasca. Want to think big, the rest of the United States lays ahead of you and you are not out of Minnesota. That is what we faced as we traveled from Seattle to Bar Harbor in 1999. This was on our first trip across the United States. We returned to Oregon in 2001 and rode to Virginia, but that comes later.

On June 3, 1999 we flew into Seattle, Washington to begin our ride east to Bar Harbor, Maine. The next day was spent visiting Seattle, Space Needle, water front, Ivar's Pier 54 Fish

Bar, and other sights. During this time, we talked to bicyclists about our ride to Anacortes, which is the kick off point for Adventure Cycling's cross-country ride from west to east. The next day we had a 6:30 breakfast appointment but it was not to be, it would be 6:45, which would cut us short for our trip to catch the ferry to Bainbridge. After debarking the ferry, we had to ride on Highway 305 which is a very busy road with a great bicycle shoulder. The sun was up, the ride was going great until, Ann had our first of twelve flats from Seattle to Bar Harbor. I could not find a cause in the tire, so a new tube and we are off for a short ride, another flat, same thing. I could not find a cause, changed the tube again and now it was raining. We were standing in front of a convenience store, so we bought a cup of instant noodles for lunch. During this time, rain, no sun, no need for sun glasses, Ann did not miss her sun glasses until we were a couple miles up the road, we returned to where she was sure she had left them, they were gone. This was our first really big crisis. Our first day turned into a night mare, lost glasses, two flats and plenty of rain. We were really pleased when we found the Aladdin Motel and began to dry out.

   By the time we had dried out it was time to eat. Across the street from the motel was a restaurant named Lonnie's. It was about 9:00 by the time we finished eating and returned to fall into bed and die! Sleep came easy that night. We were up by 5:30 with coffee first, then pack, load the bicycles and head to Keystone on Whidbey Island. From the Aladdin Motel the road was flat and no rain. Although the sky looked as if you could ring water out of the clouds. We rode through Port Townsend, a very quaint town. About this time we met two guys headed for Fidalgo Island on a training ride as they were planning to ride in France during the summer. Rick and his partner gave us some helpful hints for our ride to Anacortes and then after checking our maps decided we did not need any further assistance.

The best part of the ride that day was crossing over Deception Pass. What a view! The bridge, one of the scenic wonders of the Pacific Northwest, is actually two spans, one over Canoe Pass to the north, and another over Deception Pass to the south. Pass Island lies between the two bridges. We were about 180 feet above the water and stopped long enough to enjoy the canoes going through the Canoe Pass which is a narrow pass just north on State Highway 20. We arrived at Virginia and Jack Haywood's home around 2:45. They were attending a grandchild's birthday party and this gave us time to wash clothes, dry the clothes and wash ourselves before they returned. We celebrated with a glass of Merlot and dinner at a local restaurant.

The next morning we were photographed by the Anacortes American, the local paper, Duncan Frazier was the publisher. Then on to meet a reporter at station KIKL, a local radio station, to be interviewed live on the air and sent on our way out of Anacortes with people honking their horns as they passed sending us east toward Bar Harbor. We are now officially on our way across the USA.

We remembered Washington state well as we rode across Washington in 1990. We knew it rains a lot, really a lot, and this trip was no different. It was raining before the day was over. By the time we rode into Rasar State Park and set up camp, it was raining. We were prepared for this trip. I brought a large sheet of visqueen, clear plastic, to tie over the camp. Our tent was dry, our bench, yes bench, was dry but who in the world set the rules in Rasar State Park that bicyclists and hikers do not need a table, so we just had a bench. The next day we headed for Concrete, Washington. Just out of town we stopped for breakfast, two eggs, hash browns, toast, steak and all cooked perfectly, and all very good down to the last bite. As we rode into Concrete the center of town was almost abandoned, store fronts were boarded up. The only businesses were several auto repair shops.

We rode Highway 20 across most of the USA and on this day we headed for Marblemount and the Washington Rainy Pass. This was a 49-mile continual grade to the summit of Mt. Washington, a dip and then back to the summit of Mt. Rainy before dropping down to Winthrop.

As we rode into Marblemount, the sky was turning black and the chance for rain continued to increase. Ann and I began to discuss stopping and decided to have lunch and think about the situation. We stopped at the Buffalo Ranch Restaurant and had a bowl of black bean soup. The weather didn't improve. We decided to get a room at the Log House Inn. It was really early but there was nothing between Marblemount and Colonial Campground. We checked in our room for $27.00 a night for two, bath down the hall and if I said the floor slanted, it did, about a 15° slant toward the street. We began to laugh as everything that would roll did and always rolled toward the street. The sky began to clear, but we were committed to the Log House Inn. We took a nap and worried about losing a day's ride but about 3:00 p.m. it began to rain and we were pleased to be in for the night. Dinner was back to the Buffalo Ranch as the rain had stopped and after dinner we went for a walk. The sign said "Trout Hatchery 1" so we thought that the "1" stood for one mile. After about a half hour walk and no hatchery, we turned back and never discovered either the hatchery or what the "1" stood for on the sign.

Along the way we discovered that Washington state had "red-necks" as well as all the states in the United States. We were told to get off the road even though we were walking along the side of the road. We were pleased we were not on our bicycles! No telling what they would have had to say about us being on the road. In 1990, when we rode with Cycle America across Washington in this part of the state, the loggers equated us with tree huggers and sprayed tacks all along the bicycle trail on the road. Just walking on the road appeared to offend some people in Washington.

The next morning we left Marblemount heading for the Colonial Campground at Lake Diablo. This is the kick off point for riding over the Washington Rainy Pass. Washington Pass, (elevation 5477 feet) and Rainy Pass (elevation 4875 feet) are two mountain passes on State Route 20. Rainy Pass is about four miles to the west of Washington Pass. Bicyclists heading east gather up at the campground in the evenings to ride the forty-nine miles the next day.

We were the first to arrive at the campground and soon other bicyclists began to arrive. First came Tom somebody and Bob Sensenig of Rochester, NY. Tom did not stay around long enough to give his last name as he was home-sick for his wife, but Bob stayed. He asked about my thoughts on his decision to stay and continue the ride, and I explained my hiking partner quit on me on the PCT. I told him that I continued and never regretted making the hike. Bob rode across the USA with many different bicyclists.

Next to arrive at camp were Amy and Rebecca, with about a dozen body piercings and as many tattoos. Then Shelly and soon afterward Scott arrived and set up camp. Ann had lost a glove earlier along our ride and VOILA, Shelly had picked it up and was proud of herself for doing so, as she returned the lost glove to Ann.

That evening we had one of our freeze-dried dinners, red-beans and rice, and the next morning we had oatmeal for breakfast before loading and heading over the passes. This would be a long day as we rode into Winthrop late in the evening. When we arrived on June 10, 1999 in Winthrop we had covered 536.2 miles. After a day off, we would ride from Winthrop to Okanogan.

The morning of June 12, came early as we headed out to ride over Loup-Loup Pass, which is just over 4,000 feet, a lot shorter than Washington Pass. The day started with a twelve-mile climb, that does not sound like much but add straight up and 90° heat and it was slow going. When we topped the first rise, we had eighteen miles to coast before the mountain jumped up again. Our rubber legs were not ready for another climb. This was six miles at 6% grade and another dip and a five-mile climb at 5% grade. This would take us into the town of Okanogan.

The campground in Okanogan was clean, the rest rooms were clean and the park was a welcoming place until a group of workers arrived, set up their tents and became a loud distraction. We had picked the VFW campground on the edge of town, heading east. That evening we cooked a freeze-dried dinner in camp as we were afraid to leave our camp with the workers hanging around and drinking.

NOTE: This was the first campground from HELL, full of drunks and loud music most of the night and lots of loud talk the drunker they became. I began to fear for Ann as she was the only woman around and the drunks were talking of needing a woman. Lucky for us this did not happen but it was a memory we could have done without. There will be others along the way that we have designated as campgrounds from HELL.

About midnight I began to shake with a chill and knew I had not drunk enough water the day before. I was dehydrated big time. You also have to eat along with drinking enough liquid and this I had not done when riding over Loup-Loup Pass. This would happen to Ann when we rode across Estonia in 2003 but for now it was my pain to deal with.

We rode out of camp early, found a grocery store and I drank a pint of orange juice just to stop the shakes. We then rode into Omak for breakfast. We ate breakfast at McGoo's, and had pancakes covered with strawberries and whip cream. That was a breakfast that would bring anyone dehydrated from the day before back to life.

That night we stayed at the Red Apple Inn in Tonasket. The next morning we ate breakfast at Don's Drive Inn and yes, there was a "good ole boys table." We were welcomed to Don's with plenty of strange looks but no conversations with the locals, they just stared and stared as we ate breakfast.

The next two days were spent riding up and up to Bonaparte Lake Resort, where we camped. We were entertained by a couple of children attempting to swim in the snow melt lake. Bonaparte Lake was surrounded by a beautiful ring of mountains. We could still see snow above us but we also knew we were going downhill in the morning. The last three days had been short such as twenty-six and twenty-eight miles. It would take longer than we had planned to reach Maine.

That day was different, and we rode sixty-six miles from Bonaparte Lake to Roosevelt Lake campground. There is a system of giving restaurants stars, well today was a Five Star ride. Most of the day was downhill, through forests, along small streams, and past algae covered ponds filled with ducks. In Crulen we ate lunch at the Cougar Corner and had a Cougar Burger. By the time we were back on the road, the temperature was in the 90's and we had gone through all of our water (6 bottles) before riding over Bolder Creek Pass. We stopped at Barstow's General Store and bought two gallons of water, filled our bottles and drank the remainder. When we returned the empty containers, the owner wanted to know if we each had drunk a gallon of water.

Almost everyone we talked to said to be sure to camp at Lake Roosevelt campground. The campground was on Kamloops Island with the greatest view of the lake and the best campsite in Washington. We rode hard all day to get to the campground, rode in and paid our fee, in a box, and began to look for this great and wonderful view. The lake was down about ten to twelve feet, the handle was removed from the water pumps and we had already paid to camp. There was no water to drink or cook with and we had to save the little water we had in our water bottles for the morning ride to WHERE? We did not know how far it would be to the next store or water. It was a completely dry campground with two smelly, dirty, and grumpy people wishing for daylight as the noise from a highway echoed across the lake. It was a trying night. The next morning a highway crew arrived and we bummed water and information. There was a motel, restaurant and water just two miles further on the road. Just our luck, we stopped just short of showers. Barney's was there before FDR Lake was created. It overlooks the Kettle River and the Kettle River Falls. We took our time eating pancakes and drinking lots of coffee.

We rode around the town of Kettle Falls on back roads into Coleville about lunch time. We were greeted as we locked our bicycles up by a local resident who told us we should go to the Co-Op for lunch. It turned out to be an all-of everything store including a lunch counter which sold the food by the pound. When we departed Coleville, it was if we knew everyone in town. They gave us a grand send off on our way up, yes up, to Beaver Lake Resort.

Twenty-four miles at this point did not appear to be much but up-hill and 90° heat took a lot out of us. We had ridden fourteen miles of the climb when we passed a house just as Mike Brassard had returned home from a full day's work at an appliance factory as a welder. His mistake was speaking to us and being so nice that we asked how much he would charge to give us a ride to Beaver Lake Resort. At first, he said he had just finished a long shift at the plant, and then, Ann said, "I am sorry." We turned to ride as Mike said "Wait a minute. There is no charge. Load your bikes and gear in the truck, and I'll drive you up to the lake." Mike was just one of many along the way who went out of their way to make our ride across the USA a real pleasure, Thanks, Mike.

We unloaded from the truck at Beaver Lake Resort, checked in and ran to the shower, clean at last after two days of hot uphill riding. This was really a resort. Our camp was perfect and the sky was full of stars and we spotted a massive satellite, the second time we had spotted it in the sky. It could only have been the International Space Station or the Russian Muir Space Station. This was the best campground we had found in Washington.

From Beaver Lake Resort to Ione is listed as fourteen miles with a warning of a four-mile steep downhill grade. We were told of this grade several times by people as we got ready for our ride to Ione. With only fourteen miles we expected to begin the descent at once. We rode rolling hills on top of the pass for seven miles before coming to a sign showing a downhill grade warning of four miles of steep decline. The road was wide, the bicycle lane was wide, the curves were a little sharp but we moved along in great fashion. We were over Tiger Pass and now we were over the North Cascades. We had the Rockies ahead but at this time we had accomplished two things: we were over the Cascades and almost across our first state.

We arrived in Ione and could not believe our eyes: a health food store in an abandoned town. We bought food and headed out of town. We had gone eighteen miles and had fifty-two miles to ride to reach Newport, our last town in Washington.

After Newport, we rode into Sand Point, Idaho. It was only a thirty-five-mile ride from Newport to Sand Point and along the way we spotted bicyclists to the right of the highway. We stopped and took a look at our map and did not see a bike path, or trail in the area. I called out to one of the riders and asked where the trail went to. He said, "What are you doing on the road?" This trail goes to Sand Point." We found a place to cross over to the trail and over Lake Pend Oreille on an old highway bridge converted into a bicycle/pedestrian path.

Upon arriving in Sand Point, we checked into a motel and were awed by the fact that cars respected bicyclists and pedestrians. We walked up to a curb and cars stopped for us to cross the street. It got to the point that when we walked to the side of a street and the cars stopped, we would cross just because they had stopped. We were so impressed we began to think of Sand Point as a place to move to later in our retirement. Sometimes we think about Sand Point and think what a mistake we made by not moving.

We took a day off in Sand Point, washed clothes and shopped for food and snacks for the next few days' rides. When in the grocery store, we asked about a place to eat dinner. The lady behind us said, "Well there's only one place you must eat in Sand Point, Ivano's." The cashier said "You had better ask her how to spell Ivano's." We did and she spelled, "I-van-hoe's." So if you are in Sand Point and someone suggests you eat at Ivano's, just look for Ivanhoe's for a very good Italian meal.

Sundays were always a good day to exit a town, but not in the case of Sand Point, as the traffic was bumper to bumper on Highway 200 along the shore of Lake Pend Oreille. Also Highway 200 had a good shoulder and then no shoulder at other times. We were looking forward to arriving in Clark Fork so we could exit SR 200 and cross the river to ride on a rural road for the next fourteen miles. When we asked for directions in Clark Fork for the road we were looking for, we were told to take the old road and cross the old bridge because of the traffic on SR 200. That is right, the old bridge would not hold up cars but it would bicycles. Even the main bridge did not appear to support bicycles but at least this one did not have bumper to bumper traffic. The crossing was unique in a way as there were two falcon nests on the top of the bridge. We laughed about the flooring of the bridge as you could look through the holes at the swift water below. The old road was quiet and beautiful to ride and enjoy. We began to spot wild animals along the way as we counted the deer and mountain goats and then Ann won the prize when she spotted a small black bear.

About eight miles into the ride from the bridge crossing, I saw a man repairing his fence and asked if we were in Montana. He said, "No, about a half mile to the state line, all that you have to do is look up and you can tell when you cross the state line, the sky gets much larger." The sign for the border was so small we almost missed the crossing. We had started taking photos of each other when we crossed into another state and did so here at the crossing into Montana. We looked up and sure enough the sky was bigger!

We rode 50.4 miles to the Good Sam Campground. From Good Sam Campground, 52.1 miles to Libby, MT. Libby 61.8 miles to Rexford. Rexford 40.1 miles to Dog Creek Campground and in between Rexford and Dog Creek, Ann met her first ever really mad turkey gobbler.

Ann has a habit of making animal noises as we ride along, such as mooing at cows, braying at donkeys, clucking at chickens and on this day, gobbling like a turkey. We were on Tobacco Road about twenty miles out of Rexford when she heard a turkey gobble in the woods along the road. She gobbled to the turkey and surprisingly he gobbled and she gobbled and so did the turkey and this went on for a while until I noticed the turkey coming out of the woods. He was in full strut mode meaning he was having nothing to do with another gobbler in his woods. As he came closer, I warned Ann that he may flog her so be careful. She said what do you mean flog? He will attack with the spurs on his legs. And just about that time he charged through the fence and began to spur the front bags on her bicycle. She began to scream get him off and then we began to ride, fast, faster, and even faster before we began to pull away from the turkey. Had he been a little lighter on his feet he might even have taken flight but he was a little heavy and so he ran until we pulled away from his pursuit.

That evening we camped at Dog Creek Campground. The camp headquarters was a good ole boy hang-out in the evenings. I went in to ask about bear bagging our food and the owner said, "Don't worry about bears, all you have to do is out run your partner, surely you can out run Ann." I said, "I can't out run her even when a wild turkey gets after her." The place broke up laughing and to a man said that "You must have been up on Tobacco Road." "Yes!" Then one of the men said "Well you've met our resident wild turkey. He has become about half domesticated and thinks he owns the creek bank; it has gotten to the point where we can't go fishing up there without having to fight him off." I wrote this story to Bill Thomas of the Commercial Appeal in Memphis, Bill rewrote the story and now we have lots of turkey paraphernalia, even a reproduction of the 1999 turkey stamp.

The next day we rode into Columbia Falls, where we met Lonnie and George Parsons. They washed our clothes, gave us real beds to sleep in for the night and drove us around on a tour of Columbia Falls. They even showed us the falls in Columbia Falls. They were man-made in downtown just to say "We really do have falls." Musette Fahy grew up with Lonnie and had let them know we would be passing through Columbia Falls. In 2002 when we rode across the USA a second time, George and Lonnie had moved to Raton Pass, NM, and drove all the way to Colorado to meet us and buy us dinner.

The day off in Columbia Falls did both of us good and a great time was had with George and Lonnie. This gave us time to relax before facing the Rockies, as they were just nineteen miles from Columbia Falls.

This was a challenge we could not overcome, the ride over The Going to the Sun Highway through Logan Pass from West Glacier to Many Glacier. Without going into great detail of how we failed the climb, as we did, we could see the summit of the pass but it was noon and the ranger informed us we had to turn back as they were going to release the campers and it would be unsafe for bicyclists to be on the road. I asked if we could just try for the summit and he said he would give us a ticket if we continued. I then asked him how much was the ticket and he said it did not matter, if I give you the ticket you will still have to turn around. We turned around and returned to West Glacier for the night.

The next morning I called George Parsons and asked if he would drive us and our bicycles to the summit. He was pleased to drive us up the Going to the Sun Highway to the summit. We knew he would not take pay, and we also knew he loved macadamia nuts, so we found a jar of macadamia nuts. When we got out of his truck at the summit, we left them in the front seat of his truck. He called out "You left your macadamia nuts." We smiled and said, "They're not ours." A big smile appeared on George's face and he drove off, heading back over the pass for Columbia Falls.

This left us only twenty-seven miles to Many Glacier and a night at the Many Glacier Lodge. It fills with snow or floods each winter so the ground floor was warped. The night was quiet and the sky was still big.

From Many Glacier, Montana we rode fifty-one miles to Waterton Lakes, Alberta, Canada. One regret is that we did not stay in the Prince of Wales Hotel. When you are traveling by bicycle for three months, you have to be frugal, so we passed up the opportunity to stay at the Prince of Wales.

Along the way we passed through free land, meaning the cattle graze on open range. Of course Ann made cow noises and the cows came out onto the road and she wanted me to rescue her, which I did in sort of a way, I hollered out Huh! Huh! Hoping they would stop their charge. Really all they wanted was to follow a couple strange animals instead of eating along the roadside. We were on a very long slow climb at this time.

When we reached the Canadian border, we were asked if we had any bear spray. We did and they took our bear spray, so camping was not an option after that and a good thing as later we discovered that bear spray only made the bear madder and would not stop the charging bear. "You have to take his credit card away in order to stop a charging bear." Those are not my words, they are the words of our host at a lodge on the Madison River. The bear spray was really stolen by the border guard as it was Canadian approved from the REI store in Seattle, Washington.

The next day we rode fifty miles in rain showers off and on all day. By the end of the day we were in Cardston. We stayed in a motel and attempted to get ready for a seventy-five-mile ride back to the USA on Canada Day, July 1. We wanted to reach Cut Bank, Montana. But as we are leaving Cardston, the streets were full of people, a parade, bar-b-ques, bands, a street dance, but we still left Cardston, another missed chance to enjoy the local fair.

The terrain turned from hills and valleys to the plains. We were about thirty miles from the Rockies and they were beautiful. The trees were thinning out and the open space was just that, open and bigger, just as the man had said at the Montana state line. "Look up, the sky gets bigger in Montana." The border crossing was closed with a sign to call a number, so we called and a lady answered, asked who we were and told us to come on back to the USA. So we went around the arms at the crossing and waved at a camera on a post beside the building at the border. We were back in the USA. Rain clouds began to form and we dressed for rain. At this point in the ride there was really no place to hide from rain as we were in the plains. We were not disappointed as it rained for about an hour and a half without letting up. We had the best Gore-Tex rain gear, pants and jackets and we were dry inside but outside we were wet. Everything we had was soaked, then the sun came out. Soon we were changing back into bicycle clothing and everything was drying.

We began to get hungry, and drops of rain began again. Then we crossed the Milk River bridge, shelter, a place to eat. We climbed down the bank and under the bridge. We saw something we did not expect, swallows, by the hundreds. There were so many nests under the bridge we thought it would crash from the weight of the mud the swallows had used to build their nests. We enjoyed all the attention the birds gave us because we made them very nervous as we sat under the bridge out of the rain.

Once we climbed out of the North Milk River Valley the sky cleared and we caught a great tailwind into Cut Bank. We covered seventy-three miles that day with the last fifteen miles at a twenty-five miles per hour.

The next day we wanted to ride more miles. We succeeded as we covered seventy miles from Cut Bank to Chester. We had a great tailwind and stopped in Devon for lunch. The place was an old bar many years ago but when we were there it was a combination of many things, ice cream, lunch, antique store, and general store, just the right place to stop. The owners had many questions as they were from Washington. During lunch a lady in her eighties came in for ice cream and began to explain how the crops were planted in the plains. The spacing of the rows and how the crops were either 8", 10" or 14" rows, meaning the distance between the rows of grain. The method was called dry farming.

With a great tailwind we reached Chester early and discovered a wonderful campground. The camp was great, covered with soft grass, but the showers needed help but worked. Dinner and breakfast were at the local restaurant, Spuds, and as usual the local folks all nodded and looked us over but no conversation.

From Chester to Havre we had the BNSF as company. They always blew their horns as they passed and we waved. As we approached Havre the sky began to clear from a day threatening to rain but no rain came. We still felt a little uneasy and decided to get a motel. This was July 3, a Saturday night and it did rain, so we had made a good decision. Sunday morning came and it was still raining so we took a day off in Havre.

Since it was Sunday and we had not attended church in a very long time, I suggested we go to church. Ann asked just how do you plan to get to church? I said I would call and ask for a ride. She began to laugh as I called the First Presbyterian of Havre and soon we had a ride to church. We arrived just in time for the start of the service. When it came time for the sermon, the pastor said, "There are two people here this morning doing something many of us would like to do, so I would like them to stand, introduce themselves and tell us their story." We did and this went on for about thirty minutes, one question was, "Were you out on Highway 2 yesterday and waved at the BNSF as it honked it's horn?" I told him we were. Then the man explained he was the engineer on that train. Also he explained how he watched many bicyclists on Highway 2 as they rode across the United States. This was followed with many questions about our ride and soon the pastor said, "We will all stop now and go down into the basement for donuts and you can continue to question Ann and Roscoe." So most of our morning in Havre was spent reliving the trip from Seattle to Havre.

From Havre we rode fifty-seven miles to Harlem, and from Harlem sixty-five miles to Sleeping Buffalo Campground. This is where we had our first pizza made by a lady up in the hills, that looked just like Red Barron pizza. I questioned the origins of the pizza but everyone in the bar, at the Sleeping Buffalo was sure I was wrong. We would encounter this pizza several times in the next few days and each time they would swear it was made by a little lady up in the hills.

The day we left Sleeping Buffalo, we caught our first great tailwind, eighty-three miles into Hinsdale with time to spare. We wanted to camp on the Milk River and as we rode into the campground we were followed by a pick-up truck. The driver asked if we planned to camp there for the night. We said, "Oh yes!" He said, "You can't." "It's raining up in the mountains and this would be under water before morning. The Milk would be out of her banks before you could get out, so go back into town and get a place to stay, go to the bar, they will find you a place to stay." So we rode into town and found the Rainbow Bar. When I asked the lady at the bar if she knew of a place, where we could stay. She said, "What's wrong with here, just put your tent up in the middle of the floor and stay the night." I told her we had to ride to Wolf Point the next day. Then she said "Go next door to the grocery and see if Mr.

Jaynas has a place you can stay." We did and he gave us the key to an abandoned gas station on the edge of town and said, "All the facilities work. In the morning, just toss the key in the front seat of my race car before you leave." We went there but as the storm approached, he arrived to check on us and said, "If this thing turns into a tornado, you can get down in the old oil pit and you will be safe." I said, "Look, if this place blows in on us and we are in the oil pit we would be there for the rest of our lives." He said, "No, everyone in Hinsdale knows you are camping here tonight and not everyone will be killed, someone will rescue you." Sure enough, the storm was the worst we had ever seen short of a tornado; the wind sent the rain straight across the plains and the Milk did get out of its' banks overnight. We were blessed by many people along the way who looked out for the two of us on our ride across the USA. We are still in touch with Scott and Lorene Jaynas. Once I called Hinsdale and discovered the Rainbow Bar and the grocery store were closed. I would like to find the man in the pickup truck and thank him for saving us from a rain storm so bad we would have been soaked through and through. Since I promised Ann that I would keep her dry if she would camp with me, I would have broken that promise that night in Hinsdale.

There are things bicyclists dream of, such as a tailwind or a really strong tailwind. The next morning our dream came true, we had a really strong tailwind. It is 83.6 miles from Hinsdale to Wolf Point and we covered this distance in less than seven hours. We were in Glasgow in less than two hours and surprised our host from the night before, Scott Jaynas and his son Anthony, when they came into the same store. We were having breakfast and they had come to Glasgow to buy bread for his store in Hinsdale. He could not believe we had covered the twenty-four miles in such a short time but tailwinds will do that when you can ride twenty-five to thirty miles per hour. The only stops we made that day were bathroom breaks and snacks as we wanted to take advantage of the wind.

That was our last day in Montana. We covered ninety-nine miles from Wolf Point to Williston, ND. We really had to push ourselves to make the distance. The first part of the ride was a piece of cake, then hills, then more hills and then road construction. The road bed was gone and only mud for the highway remained. There are kind people in this world, and we were given a ride across the construction zone on the back of a low-boy trailer, towed by a large tractor.

If you want to know where the buffalo roam, well in the hills west of Williston, and if you want to know about skunks, they were along the highway as you approach Williston. Looking back, I wish I had stopped long enough to photograph the many skunks along this part of Highway 2. But at this point into the ride, we had stopped taking photos, and rode with our heads down, looking for a motel at the end of a very long day. The Super 8 would do, so we checked in for the night.

After two long days of riding we took the next day off, one to rest, one to clean our bicycles and to get them ready for the next phase of the ride. We took our bicycles to Coast-to-Coast Hardware, for a cleaning and oiling and then we went to Kathey's for haircuts. I bought a pin shaped like a fish for Ann and our granddaughter Lilly while Ann browsed the local book store. I began to talk to a local and he in turn asked what we were doing for the day in Williston. "Nothing!" Then he introduced himself. Bruce Conway and his wife, Bev, they asked Ann and me to join them for a day of sight-seeing around Williston. First, we went to Fort Buford for a reenactment, then to Fort Union, and last to Epping, ND, for bar-be-que, ND style. Epping was a town of dirt streets, wooden sidewalks and looked more like a movie set for a western movie than a real town. At the end of the day we were very tired and had not rested for the next day's ride. We returned, rescued our bicycles and rode back to the Super 8 for the night.

The next day we only rode 25.2 miles to Lunds Landing on Lake Sakakawea. We ate walleye for dinner at Lunds Landing and checked into the lodge, well not really a lodge, the facilities were down the road, as well as the showers. During the night when it was time to make a run to the facilities, to the north we saw the sight of sights, the Northern Lights! We could hardly believe our eyes. The beauty of dancing lights on the northern sky will make you smile from ear to ear and laugh out loud as you marvel at the wonders of the night sky.

From Lake Sakakawea we rode 58 miles to Parshall and 70.8 miles to Minot, just as we reached Minot, two tornados hit the town shortly after we checked into a Super 8 Motel, we felt very blessed.

Minot 49.2 miles to Towner, and a surprise, a cheese factory. We bought cheese from the factory and went to the local grocer for grapes, and crackers and then to a wonderful park to enjoy our purchases. Well, almost wonderful, no showers. But we could make one night without a shower, or could we? Just as we were setting up our tent a gentleman walked into the park and began to ask how we liked the park? I asked him if he was the mayor? "Why, yes." "I am." He introduced himself, "I'm Steven Foster." Then we introduced ourselves and Ann explained it was great but no showers. He then put his arm around Ann's shoulder and pointed to a house: "Little lady, you see that green house, you be there at 6:00 and you can have a shower." I asked if his wife knew he was inviting strangers for a shower and he said, "I'm single and you are welcome to come to my house for a shower." In one afternoon we met the mayor of Towner, Steven Foster, not bad for a town in North Dakota to have a mayor with such a famous name.

We invited Mayor Foster to dinner and the three of us returned to town and had dinner at the Ranch House Restaurant. All was well, shower and dinner with Steven Foster and now it was time to crawl into the tent for the night. Wrong, about 3:00 a.m. thunder and lightning flashed. We pulled up the tent, and moved into the picnic shelter, bikes and all as quickly as we could and yes, it was another strong rain storm, but we had a dry place to spend the rest of the night.

The next day was wet as it rained all day. We rode to Rugby, which is the Geographic Center of North America. We arrived early, cold and wet, showered to get warm, took a nap and prepared for a long day to Devils Lake. That evening we walked into town and the local bank was celebrating their 102 years in business. We had free hot dogs, baked beans and all the trimmings.

From Rugby it is 82.3 miles to Devils Lake. If you have never read, heard or seen Devils Lake, you need to do so. We did not know anything about the lake or what was going on in that part of ND. The lake was coming up from the bottom, flooding everything in that part of ND. The highway was below the lake, with a levee on each side of the highway. We rode through the lake. When I say through the lake, the lake was above us as we rode along looking over the levee and wondering if it would hold back the water. The towns around the lake were drowning as the lake continued to rise. It was a study in the effect of nature.

We rode on from Devils Lake 67.2 miles to Binford, and 45.0 miles to Hope. It was spitting rain when we arrived in Hope and a couple stopped us to ask about our ride. We asked if there was any place to rent a room and the couple told us to go to Geraldine Jacobson's house, last house on the left on Main Street. The couple said, "Tell her, Jack and Joyce Germanson sent you, she is a delight." When she answered the door and we asked about the room, she said, "Yes, the postal lady will not be here until Monday, so the room is for rent." Then she asked if $20.00 was ok? I had to hold a straight face and say of course. We rented the room and asked her out to lunch, she declined, when we went to the Roadrunner Restaurant we understood why, the food was over cooked and impossible to eat. We complained but the food was what it was, and we picked at the pork chop we had ordered, paid, and returned to Mrs. Jacobson's. Dinner that night was pb&j with Mrs. Jacobson as she told us many stories about North Dakota.

A side note: We corresponded with Mrs. Geraldine Jacobson until we received a letter from her son informing us, she had passed away. This correspondence lasted from Christmas 1999 until 2014. She always wanted to know where we had traveled by bicycle each year and we kept her up to date. She was a kind lady who took us in out of the rain, as did so many people we met along the way.

Morning came at 6:00 a.m. and we were loaded and off by seven with the blessings of Mrs. Jacobson. We stopped by the Bowling Cafe for breakfast. Pancakes, two for two dollars, and we are off by 7:45 riding like the wind and made fourteen miles in less than an hour. We stopped in Page, ND to pick up snacks for the ride. Page had created parking like every city in the USA dreams about. The main street was so wide that the cars parked head to head in the middle of the street and head in to the curb with plenty of space to drive through town. What a great method of parking!

We left Page with cherries and apples and headed for Fargo. We arrived in Fargo by 4:00 p.m. and checked into a hotel in downtown, showered, dressed and headed to the O&B Brewery for a beer. We discovered Luigi's located at the Conservatory and had dinner.

People in North Dakota told us the state was flat from Williston to Fargo, and people who have driven across North Dakota have also told us the state is flat, well they have never been to Lake County in Tennessee. Lake County is flat, North Dakota is rolling, now the roads are straight, but it is a long way from flat. If anyone wants to see flat come to Lake County in Tennessee and you will see flat.

After a day off in Fargo we rode 63 miles to Maple Wood Campground in Minnesota. We had now covered over 2,000 miles without a major breakdown, that would change, as we were leaving the Maple Wood Campground. Something caught in my derailleur and twisted it into a knot along with breaking the chain. With a loaded bicycle and no way to roll it back into camp, we unloaded, and carried everything back to the camp headquarters and asked if the owner would drive us back to Fargo to a bicycle shop. He informed us of a bicycle shop in Detroit Lakes and that his wife had a dental appointment that morning and if we could wait, he would drive us to the bike shop. We waited, and he dropped us off at the shop. The Caprice Motel was behind the bike shop, we checked into the motel and returned to the shop to be told he did not have any derailleur for our bicycles. I called Outdoors, Inc. in Memphis and had Joe Royer FedEx the part to Detroit Lakes. The next day the part arrived, the owner of the shop and I replaced the derailleur and the broken chain. After a two day delay, and dry nights, as it rained both nights that we were stranded, we departed Detroit Lakes and headed to Tamarac Lake Campground, just a 31-mile ride.

One of the bright spots along the way were the bald eagles at the lakes. Once, while we were stopped near a lake the loons were very noisy and I asked a man why were the loons making so much noise. He pointed to the top of a tree and said "If you were about to be dinner you would make noise too." When I looked up, sitting in the top of the tree was a bald eagle. The man stated, "Loons are their favorite food."

From Tamarac Lake Campground, we rode 75 miles to Bemidji, the home of Paul Bunyan. But first things first, we wanted to wade across the Mississippi River at the head waters of Lake Itasca State Park. This we did and then headed south down the Great River Road toward Minneapolis, about five days away by bicycle.

We had seen lots of wild animals along our ride but there in Minnesota we saw many different animals, deer, coyote, otters and eagles. The outdoors is a great place and add wild animals, Ann was on top of the world. We stopped to enjoy each one on our ride into Bemidji.

We had four days to ride to Minneapolis with a 46-mile, 71-mile, 73 mile and a nice 13-mile day from Anoka to Minneapolis, our shortest day. We were house guests of Lee Ann and Sandy Ridgway, they are first cousins on my mother's side of the family. What a treat, as we were given a party and a dessert in the shape of the USA with layers of red, white and blue.

We left Minneapolis July 31, 1999 after two days off and decided to head north across Wisconsin to beat the heat. We rode over fifty miles on bicycle paths through Minneapolis and north to William O'Brian State Park along the Saint Croix River, on the Minnesota and Wisconsin border. We camped in the state park and headed into Wisconsin on August 1. We rode sixty-seven miles to Cumberland, Wisconsin and stayed in the Lakeview Motel. We ordered pizza delivered and the owner of the motel gave us a couple beers to go with the pizza. I'm not saying we were tired but we slept twelve hours. From Cumberland we rode to Haywood a distance of sixty miles.

Haywood has it all, it is home of the largest cross-country ski race in North America, home of the Fresh Water Fish Hall of Fame and home of the Lumber Jack World Championship. We attended the lumberjack competition that evening and laughed at the largest walleye fish in the world, well it's a building made to look like a fish and painted to appear to be a walleye. We rode from Haywood to Glidden for a fifty-four-mile day and then on to Bolder Junction at sixty-five miles the next day. We crossed into Michigan somewhere between Bolder Junction and Crystal Falls. We rode eighty-five miles that day and then seventy-five the next day into Escanaba. Once we were in Michigan, we began to stretch the miles each day in order to reach St. Ignace and take a day off to visit Mackinaw Island. Never plan to bicycle on Mackinaw Island. Take a day off and enjoy watching people who haven't ridden a bicycle in years struggle to ride. Take a buggy ride and enjoy lunch at the fort overlooking downtown Mackinaw.

After a day off and some creative map reading, we decided to head north to Sault Ste. Marie and cross northern Ontario, Canada. The bridge over the Sea-way was imposing, rising up high over the waterway to allow the ships and barges to pass below. So Ann began to worry about riding across the bridge into Canada. This went on all evening and late into the night, with me attempting to assure her it was doable, but it did not calm her fears. Finally I gave up and called the bridge to find out if it was open to bicyclists. The man on the phone asked, "What is the problem?" I again repeated my question as to whether the bridge was open to bicyclists. He again asked, "What is the problem? Bicyclists ride over the bridge every day so what is the problem?" The next morning we loaded and rode over the bridge into Canada followed by a long line of trucks with forty-two wheels loaded with pulp-wood.

NEVER DO THIS, NEVER RIDE HIGHWAY 17

This was our most dangerous highway to ride on the entire trip. If you have ever ridden with 42 WHEEL trucks at 90 MPH (the trucks not us) then you understand what highway 17 from Sault Ste. Marie to Escanaba, Ontario, Canada was like. We were two happy bicyclists when we left highway 17 and headed south on highway 6 to Manitoulin Island. Along the way we stayed in Thessalon on Lake Huron, watched the sun set and enjoyed a wonderful restaurant and motel but it wasn't worth the ride along highway 17.

We slept in Little Current on Manitoulin Island, after passing all the traffic waiting for a swinging bridge. The trouble was that the driver in the lead car was sound asleep. With a one lane bridge and no traffic we didn't wake him. We rode across the bridge and looked back. The Royal Canadian Police also wanted to know why the traffic wasn't moving and woke the driver from his nap. We pulled off the road as the irate drivers sped past.

The next day, August 13, we woke up to a pouring rain. We decided to ride back roads to avoid the heavy traffic across the island on highway 6. We rode fifty miles and raced to catch the ferry across Lake Huron at 1:30 p.m. We made it to the ferry just as the sky opened up. It rained so hard, that we were soaked even through our rain gear. We dried out under the hand dryer in the ferry rest rooms. We had a two-hour ferry ride south. When we left the ferry, we found a festival going on and no rooms or campground within twenty miles of Tobermory. So we hurried off to the closest B&B and a wonderful evening with dinner at the Rocky Raccoon Restaurant, a kind land lord, a washing machine and a barn to dry our clothes in out of the rain.

The next day we entered the tranquil rural area of Ontario, and camped in Scone. Then on to St. Jacobs in the heart of the Mennonite country of Canada. From St Jacobs we rode south and we were told we would have to pass Ayre, (that is pronounced Air) in order to reach Paris. Well, we found Ayre to be a wonderful town, with a beautiful park and friendly people. We were interviewed by the local newspaper as we passed Ayre on our way to Paris. Then to Brantford as there were no rooms in Paris. The next day we found a rails to trail bike path from Brantford to Hamilton. In Hamilton we lost the trail and ended up riding on Main street through Hamilton. It was somewhat like riding Poplar Avenue in Memphis, Tennessee at rush hour but with much kinder drivers. We never felt threatened, just pushed along as we rode. We were looking for a bicycle path from Hamilton to Niagara Falls. We found the trail, camped in a conservation area called Fifty-six Point and then into Niagara On The Lake the next day. This is the home of the Shaw Festival; these are plays written during George Bernard Shaws' life time but not necessarily by him. There were three theatres with productions going on all day. Ann and I took a day off to enjoy Arthur Millers', "All My Sons". The next day we rode into Niagara Falls and enjoyed the tourist things, such as a ride on the "Maid of the Mist".

After a couple days rest, we crossed into New York. New York has the best kept secrets in the USA. When they mark a bicycle route, there are wide shoulders, and they are clean. I would say the best state to ride in is New York. Also they have the Erie Canal Bicycle Path. This is the old tow path along the Erie Canal. We rode over one-hundred miles from Locksport to Palmyra. What a wonderful asset for them to use for recreation. I could write a book about the towns we passed through along the Erie Canal, but I must get along at this time and tell you the Adirondack Mountains lay ahead.

We had been warned by the riders we met going east to west that we had rough riding ahead. Well, as Ann and I would reach the top of each climb we would wonder where was that big bad climb we were told about. We made the Adirondack Mountains just fine. In fact on one strip of highway we had the road to ourselves. You see a trailer truck loaded with boats attempted to turn into a driveway in a curve, the trailer caught on the bottom side and blocked the highway and also blocked the train track. Ann and I just pushed around all the confusion and rode off on a highway full of west bound cars wondering what had happened ahead.

We still had the Green Mountains in Vermont and the White Mountains in New Hampshire ahead of us. We were in our middle ring over Kancamagus Pass in New Hampshire. Well, I can tell you, I'd loved to have been in Ione, Washington when they started up Tiger Pass if these were big bad climbs. I suppose we did get stronger as we rode and also these passes were a lot shorter in miles than out west.

Sound like I'm bragging, well, we hadn't reached Maine yet. Our first day in Maine we would climb up just to fly back down to the bottom of another dip. The dips always had a short twelve percent grade waiting for us and at the end of our first day in Maine, Ann and I were ready to turn around and look for another ending. We had ridden too far to give up now but believe me Maine was a tester. The second day was a little better and the third day we felt we were going to win.

When we reached Augusta and the Gardner KOA, we were surprised with company from Germantown, Tennessee, George and Phyllis Kelly. They had the list of places we would stay and the dates when we thought we would be at that location. They were parked in the campground waiting for our arrival. George helped me set up the tent, unload the bicycles, lock everything down and then the four of us were off to eat lunch at a restaurant which was located in a former morgue. Then on into Augusta and a visit to the Capital of Maine. They could not do enough for us, and wanted to be sure we had everything we needed at the camp.

That evening George called the Germantown Presbyterian Church to let them know we were in Maine and had one more day of riding before we reached the Atlantic Ocean, 4,395.8 miles. Sunday morning Earnest Mellor, one of the pastors at the church, announced our accomplishment to the congregation and we were told the church broke into an applause for us on that Sunday morning. We knew we were on top when we stopped for breakfast in Ellsworth the next morning. When we started to pay, and we were told the breakfast was on the house, for riding from coast to coast. Thirty miles later we reached Bar Harbor and dipped our front tires in the North Atlantic on 9-9-99 at 2:22 p.m. How did we feel? Did you ever receive just what you wished for Christmas? This was the day we received our dream for ten years all at once. We rode our bicycles from coast to coast.

When we flew to Seattle on Delta, we also had a ticket home from Bar Harbor, and as the plane approached the Memphis airport the Flight Attendant came on the air and announced that we had just ridden our bicycles across the USA. We received a roaring applause, a lot of thumbs up, and the well wishes from the other passengers. This ride just proved to us what we can do, so we decided to go to Europe, land in Amsterdam, ride to the south of France and back to Amsterdam. This we did in 2000. We have never stopped looking for great adventures.

2000 From Amsterdam to Amsterdam
By way of Belgium, France and back to Amsterdam, (using two books listed below)

"Cycling The Netherlands, Belgium, and Luxembourg"
By: Katherine and Jerry Whitehill, 1998
Pages 89 and 90 Route 2 (SN1)

Part I: **"France by Bike"**
Part II: "14 Tours Geared for Discovery"
by: Karen and Terry Whitehill
A list of Tours in the order we rode them: Tour No. 4, Tour No. 11, Tour No. 5, Tour No. 3, Tour No. 2, and Tour No. 1
We returned to France in 2001 and completed many of the other tours.

Our first three days were spent in Amsterdam and Haarlem. This was my first time in Europe. The surprise came as we arrived at Schiphol Airport. When we rode out of the airport on our bicycles, dressed in our Memphis Hightailer's jerseys, a young man flagged us down and asked if we were really from Memphis. "Yes!" He was from Cordova, Tennessee and worked for Fedex. He wanted to know how he could purchase a Memphis Hightailer's jersey. He said he would call his mother in Memphis and have her send the jersey to him. I suppose he did. Then he sent us on along the bicycle path toward Haarlem. We got turned around and had to ask a lady on a bicycle which path to take, she said "follow me," and we did, as we approached an underpass she said "You will have to ride fast as we have to make a climb." We rode through an underpass with a bicycle ledge on which to ride making it half as deep as underpasses in the USA. Later Ann and I laughed about the underpasses and having to ride fast to go up hill. Dutch bikes have no gears. This was our first ride in the Netherlands and we rode 17 kilometers to reach Haarlem.

The next two days we did tourist things, visited the Van Gogh Museum, Ann Frank's house, took a boat ride on the canals around Amsterdam and just played. This was an attempt to reset our clocks after the flight over from Memphis. On our first night in Haarlem we looked for a restaurant away from a lot of tourists. We found the De Gekroonde Hamer restaurant in Haarlem. We were seated on the roof of the building and had a quail dinner along with the locals, no tourists, and a wonderful evening in Haarlem.

Each trip Ann and I take I decide to write my thoughts along the way. When I read a travel journal, it is always about a person searching for themselves. I am not. I know where I am, and I am pleased to look across the table from me and see Ann, and know I always want to be with her. I enjoy our lives together and wish for this life forever.

I do not ride my bicycle to prove my speed or ability, I ride to see the beauty of the surrounding country. So tomorrow we will start our ride south across the Netherlands. I don't want to turn this into a right and left turn mileage chart of our travels but to tell the stories of the people we talked with and the places we visited. Our first place to visit after leaving Haarlem was Keukenhof Gardens. The tulips were mostly gone but lots of other flowers were open, more than enough to see and to keep us busy most of the day. By the time we left the Gardens we needed a place to camp. We had read about a campground close to the Gardens but reading a bicycle map to the campground became an operation.

We were standing in the road outside of the Gardens, when a farmer on his tractor stopped to see if we needed instructions.

"Yes! We need directions to this campground," "No you don't want to go there when you can camp at my farm, plenty of grass to camp on, safe, quiet, and warm showers, what more can you ask for?" "Sure," so we followed his tractor along the way to the farm. He then gave us a tour of the farm and farm animals, such as the "man" cow. "I said bull!" "He said" "Man cow" so we settled on man cow. He was correct it was the nicest campground we stayed in on this trip. We rode into Warmond that evening for dinner and discovered everything was closed, except the Elephant Club, a tennis and golf club. They were serving dinner, so we ate dinner at the Elephant Club in Warmond.

From his farm we rode to Leiden then to Delft, where we needed help finding the VVV (tourist information center). There we were guided by an Auberge truck and half of the town to the VVV. After finding a place to stay we took a walk to the town hall. As we entered a couple of men our age were sitting on a bench waiting for court to open and they asked, "Where are you from in the states?" "Tennessee!" "Oh, that's where they do not believe in evolution." The "Scopes Monkey Trial," half way around the world and that is what Tennessee is known for, "We do not believe in evolution."

We took the next day off to visit The Hague, home of the Peace Palace and Madurodam a miniature park and tourist attraction in the Scheveningen district of The Hague in the Netherlands. It is home to a range of 1:25 scale model replicas of famous Dutch landmarks, and historical cities. Ok, so it is a tourist trap but you can see a lot of Holland in a hurry and also visit the candy factory which makes Mars Bars, (no longer made in the USA). It has a coin operated truck which ran over to the factory, backed into the loading dock, a Mars Bar was dropped into the bed of the truck and it brought the candy bar back for the owner to take out of the truck and enjoy. Which we did. As a matter of fact several years ago Ann and I spent many breaks eating an apple and Mars Bar along the side of the road as we rode across the USA in 1999.

The next day we rode into Gouda. As we crossed the town square a television crew came running over to where we had stopped and the lady stuck the microphone in my face and said, "You look so sporty, what makes you look so sporty?" Ann and I looked at each other dumb founded as to what to say and the interview began anew with the same question, "You look so sporty, what makes you look so sporty?" We began to laugh and explained that we had just arrived in Holland from the USA and did not understand the question. This changed everything and the travel questions began as to where we were from and where we were going. We explained our summer travels and the reporter and crew were in awe that we planned to ride our bicycles that far. In most of Europe, the bicycle is used to ride around town, not to travel long distance.

After riding a week in The Netherlands, we headed for Belgium. Along the way we visited many wind mills. Each one was unique in its own way, but they all grind the grain. All of the ones we visited were working mills. The area is known as Kinderdijk, and the picture postcard of Dutch windmills. When we crossed the Beneden Merwede River, on a foot ferry, we stopped for lunch and admired the barge traffic as barge after barge steamed past.

I thought summer was over in The Netherlands as it was raining almost all day every day and this one was no different as we are soaked through and through. We were lucky to have new bright yellow Gore Tex rain gear from Pearl Izumi and we were dry.

We soon arrived in Breda and as usual we went straight to the VVV to find a room. We had really discovered a wonderful method of finding a place to stay. The rooms were usually under $40.00 US for two, now remember this was in 2000 and before the Euro. Like the saying goes, "The worst day of biking is better than the best day at work." Well this was just about the worst day of biking because we rode in the rain most of the day.

After crossing into Belgium we found camping villages to rent small cabins. These were very basic as we used our own camping gear and sleeping bags on the bunk beds. The toilet and showers were a distance away but the place was clean and cheap. Oh! How cheap, they were less than $20.00 US and again this was in 2000. The book we were using to guide us across The Netherlands and Belgium had a lot of great suggestions as to where to stay, eat and places to visit. We took a day off and visited Brussels by train and returned in the afternoon.

Several days later we crossed the border between Belgium and France, still raining, but just maybe we would ride out of the rain. When we rode into the town of Signy-l'Abbaye, France, Ann had had enough riding in the rain and cold for one day. It was about eleven o'clock in the morning and she stated: "I don't care if a hotel does not have a star we are stopping." It did not have a star! It looked like it had not rented a room in months but it was a hotel and we could get out of the rain. We stopped, rented a room and put everything away. Security for the bicyclette (bicycles) and yes, they were pleased to store the bicyclettes and all was wonderful.

Then we walked up the street to a restaurant, which just so happened to be an Auberge. An Auberge is a French word for an inn, and can also be a restaurant or combination of both. This was both and an excellent one at that, clean and a great lunch, just the kind of place Ann had envisioned for us to stay as we rode into Signy-l'Abbaye. Now she wanted to change hotels. She explained to me that we could complain about the bathroom and that would give us the excuse to leave. She also explained how she would use her French to explain why we must "go," meaning we had to move to the Auberge.

So in Ann's French she said to the owners wife, "tu dois partir" which came out, "you must leave," instead of we must leave, "nous devons partir." The shock on the ladies face was just that shock, great shock and then Ann began to attempt to reword her statement and finally said it in English, which our host understood. Then she led us up a set of stairs to a brand-new bathroom completely refurnished. So we did not move to the Auberge.

We were entertained that afternoon with a funeral service at a small church across the street from the hotel. The guests were decked out in regal attire and the men with sashes across their chests. It was a spectacle to behold. We took a nap and later decided to return to the Auberge for dinner.

Now you must understand we only have a limited dress code, black rain pants, yellow rain jacket and of course tennis shoes. Along the way I had taken a flyer from a utility pole and had it folded in my pocket. We received a different welcome than when we had arrived for lunch. The funeral crowd was there and we were placed in a far corner of the restaurant. I told Ann that I think we should order a beer and see how the service turns out, it turned out just as we thought, we did not exist. So we sat, drank our beer and thought about what to do next. Just about that time a server made up our minds for us, she spilled a large tray of apéritifs on a table of about twelve from the funeral. That is a very sweet drink, that is also very sticky, we made the mistake of laughing. I told Ann we better go. We got up to pay and as we were leaving, I asked, "Where is this?" and brought out the flyer. With her nose in the air she said, "You do not want to go there."

I looked at Ann and said "This is where we need to go." So we began to walk around looking for "le Festival des Cafes," (The Coffee Festival) advertising a concert on Saturday, May 27, 2000. Danwez Mad would be featured at 10:00 p.m. at Café le Cerf d'Or (The Golden Deer Cafe). As Ann and I continued to walk and look for the festival, we turned a corner and the street was full of people. Our kind of people, as they were not dressed to attend the funeral. So we began to walk toward the crowd and suddenly the crowd parted as if Moses had parted the Red Sea, and out came a lady motioning for us to come and saying, "Come-come we want you to sit at the bar." Our bright yellow jackets had caught her eye and so we became a part of the festival. We were given two Kronenbourg 1664 bottles of beer and instructed that the 1664 would be facing the camera, yes, we were being filmed along with the slapstick actors and actresses as they performed in what we found out later that evening was a new movie coming out later in 2000. We never did get the name of the movie but we enjoyed the beer that evening. When the show was over, I took the poster over to the performers and they all autographed it. We have the poster hanging in our den and someday maybe we will return it to Signy-l' Abbaye, France.

From Signy-l' Abbaye it became a ride in the rain or sit it out, we rode thinking we could find a place in Europe were it was not raining. When we reached Reims, France we met our first "Flim-Flam man." He met us with a wonderful greeting and asked if we needed a hotel? Yes, but we want to be more in the middle of the city near the Cathedral of Reims. "Oh no! Just down the street is a wonderful hotel, the Hôtel de Ville." That is when I called to Ann and said "Ride-ride we have a "Flim-Flam man." Of course he protested and we let him know that the Hôtel de Ville is the city hall. As we entered the city square, we found many hotels and settled down in sight of the Cathedral of Reims. That evening we treated ourselves to dinner in an open-air restaurant without rain. We ordered the tower of the sea, "tour de la mer." It was a tower from a large round base and each level became smaller as it reached higher and higher. The top level held the small snails and the bottom started with the lobster claws, in between, each level was different kinds of shell fish until as I said at the top were the small snails. The tools were everything from a pair of pliers to a small nettle. We had a blast eating great sea food in the shadow of the Cathedral of Reims. This was where all the Kings of France had been crowned from the days of Clovis of the Franks.

We took a day off in Reims to enjoy playing tourist, exploring the caves of the G.H. Mumm, Cordon Rouge Brut, Champagne cellars. Mumm's Cordon Rouge was Humphrey Bogart's favorite champagne. I had used a line in the musical "Applause," "Come on up to my place, I have a bottle of Mumm's Cardon Rouge cooling on ice." So I really wanted a taste of his favorite champagne and we did. Also during WW II, when Reims was bombed the people of Reims had taken the stain glass windows out of the Cathedral and stored them in the caves under the city, so the windows were kept in the Mumm's cellars and after the war the original stained glass was returned to the Cathedral and they were still beautiful.

We returned to the trip we had planned from home to ride in a circle from Amsterdam and back to Amsterdam, riding south to France, then west across France to le Mont St. Michel, then back through Brugge Belgium to Amsterdam. This would have been a perfect plan and great ride but for rain.

When we arrived in Epernay, it continued to rain, we thought we could ride out of the rain by heading south. This was another one of those bad decisions. By noon we had ridden about 15 kilometers when I had a flat in the small town of Le

Mesnil-sur-Oger. I pushed the bicycle to a cover in front of Le Mesnil Restaurant. We decided to eat lunch and then fix the flat. As we walked into the restaurant, the owner welcomed us almost as family. She took our very wet coats and hung them up for us, seated us at a very nice table. All was great, as we were out of the rain and treated like royalty. The lunch would last for about two hours, with white asparagus, noodles and salmon a fromage (cheese) tray, and a dessert tray.

As we sat at the table a gentleman came over, introduced himself and stated "That at the table where he was seated were all salesmen for Mumm's winery." He gave us his card just in case we came to Paris. We were to give him a call, he would love to talk to us about our trip through Europe. By this time we realized we could not ride out of the rain and needed help. I had to fix the flat and sent Ann to check out a B&B which she found closed and returned to let me know we had to find another place to stay. The owner of a garage and gas station had been kind enough to allow me to change the tire inside the garage. With a lot of hand signals I showed him the fold-up tire and attempted to explain the reason we were having so many flats, because of the cobblestone streets. He began to attempt to let me know that Specialized Bicycle made a bicycle tire that would stand up to the cobblestones and cut down on having flats. He wrote down the word Armadillo and indicated this was the tire I needed to avoid the problem of flats. He also directed me to a bicycle shop in town. We replaced the tires we brought from home with the Armadillo tires, and we did not have another flat that summer.

When we asked about a place to stay, he said we would have to return to Epernay, about 15 kilometers back the way we had come, and in the rain. Enough is enough, there must be some place in France it is not raining and the sun is shining. So we are going south until we find such a place, by train, bus or car it did not matter. We are going to dry out somewhere in France.

First to the La Gare (train station), no trains with baggage cars for bicycles. No busses with cargo space for bicycles, oh, but car rental is just across the street from the bus station. We walked over and asked about renting a car, it must be a one-way rental, and it must be large enough for two bicycles and panniers. They had such a car! The Fiat Multiply, it was a six-passenger car with three bucket seats in from and three bucket seats in the second row with luggage space behind the rear seats and here was the kicker! The rear seats would stand up straight when you pushed on them, leaving all the space where they had been plus the luggage area. We only had to remove the front wheels and the bicycles would fit in the car from side to side. We placed all the bags in the car and we are off looking for the part of France where it was dry.

We drove for 10 hours as fast as allowed except for the first toll booth. I drove up and the arm was across the entrance, I began to check out the machine for a place to pay, no slots, and then Ann said, "Just throw the money in the basket and when it rolls out the bottom the arm will open." I was a little smarter. I realized that it was a trash basket, not a place to throw money. We sat at the booth for quite a while until a car rolled up behind us. I thought this was simple, just ask how to get on to the A&E, (the interstate highway). I walked back to the car and he sat with his window closed, but I asked anyway, and he just sat, I asked in my best French if he spoke English and he sat. I thought well, if you want on the A&E bad enough you will help me figure out what I have to do to get the arm to open. Soon a lorry (large truck) pulled up behind him, so I began to walk back to the lorry, when suddenly he rolled down his window and shouted loud and clear in perfect English with a British accent, "Punch the red button and take the ticket you dumb son-of-a-bitch." I began to laugh and said, "I certainly improved your English." Then I noticed the red button and pushed it and out came the ticket, pulled it out, the gate opened and we headed south to Avignon.

France was dry! There was a place in France where it did not rain all summer and we found just the place, southern France. We had to return the car at the airport and found it after much searching, found a motel near the airport as we rode toward Avignon, checked in, cleaned the bicycles, loaded them so we would be ready to ride the next morning.

June 1, 2000, a national holiday had been declared, nothing was open and again we needed a little help getting through Avignon. Avignon is one of the most difficult cities to bicycle through that we have ever encountered. The old and new are separated by a wall and finding the entrance to the old part of the city from the new is a challenge, we made it and then to the Rhone River. We stopped for photos of the old city; the famous bridge that was never completed across the Rhone which Van Gogh made famous in one of his paintings. Then we headed north to Pont-Saint-Esprit. As we crossed the Rhone we met two bicyclists and I asked, "Do you speak English?" and the reply was, "We are English." We all had a laugh and then found that everything going north to Pont-Saint-Esprit was closed. We had a couple apples and it wasn't that far, so we decided to tough it out one day to reach Pont-Saint-Esprit.

The English were wrong. We discovered a town about half way to Pont-Saint-Esprit, where a cafe was open, with open air seating and great service. The owner enjoyed having two American travelers stop at his cafe and in broken English and broken French we laughed and ordered lunch. All he had was some kind of meat, he took me into the kitchen and pointed,

I took a look and knowing lamb, I said "Baa?" He said "No, BAA-BAA," and I knew it was mutton. We ordered as Ann and I both like lamb. The French know how to cook and lunch was again a two-hour affair, salad, mutton, cheese tray, and dessert, nothing is simple when eating out in France. We fell in love with the lazy days.

As we approached Pont-Saint-Esprit, we saw a sign pointing toward the Rhone River, advertising a camp ground. Great we can camp tonight, clear sky, and warm. Not so, as we headed to the camp ground, Ann spotted a sign for a "Country Inn." She wanted to just ride up to the Inn and see what it was like, I knew what it was like, it was like we are not going to camp on the Rhone River that night and we did not camp.

This Country Inn was built in the 1400's making it almost 600 years old, stately, and just the place for a couple of bicyclists to stay, except it was six miles from Pont-Saint-Esprit and the sign stated breakfast included. No dinner without a six-mile ride in and six miles back out to the Country Inn. Well, things do work out as the owners must have been very hungry for people to stay at their Country Inn. When we started to leave because there was no DINNER, the owner asked if we would mind eating with him and his family. "No, we would love to eat with you." Under any circumstance, that would save a 12-mile bicycle ride this late in the day. So, we checked into the Country Inn.

There was a swimming pool, indoor tennis court and our room was large enough that we could ride our bicycles across the room and park them on a bicycle stand. There was a covered area for breakfast but for dinner that evening there was a table set up for 12 under a very large sycamore tree. We were introduced to the family, his wife, three girls, two boys and three workers. Everyone spoke English, and the questions were about our trip in Europe. Then I asked how such a young couple were able to acquire such a beautiful chateau?

He said, his grandfather had a friend in the US by the name of Garcia, and his grandfather sent him an open-face fishing reel and asked if he would check it out and see if it would really work. Mr. Garcia did just that, it worked, we were eating at the table of Mitchell for which the Garcia/Mitchell fishing reel was named and that is how he was able to acquire the chateau. Then he asked if we enjoyed the shade of the sycamore tree? We did and then he said, "The original owners of the chateau were hung from the limbs of the tree during the French Revolution." Well that was a long time ago and we did enjoy our evening. The next morning breakfast was served in the open dining area outside our room, the usual, bread, butter and jam.

The next day as we departed we had company on our ride into Pont-Saint-Esprit, three girls and two boys on their way to school. At a fork in the road the children made a great fuss over saying good-byes and we were again alone heading over the Gorges de l'Ardèche. The Gorges de l'Ardèche is made up of a series of gorges in the river and locally known as the "European Grand Canyon," Located in the Ardèche, in the French department Ardèche, forming a thirty-kilometre long canyon running from Vallon-Pont-d'Arc to Saint-Martin-d'Ardèche. Along the way we had to ride through a very long tunnel, lighted, but never the less a tunnel. The good side of it was we were on the downhill side when we reached the tunnel. On our way up, we met bus loads of tourists. As the busses approached us their hands would come out of the windows and the applause would start as they passed me and continued until they realized the second rider was a woman, then the cheers would erupt from the bus. The end was the ah ha moment of the day. We arrived at the most wonderful natural arch over the Ardeche River, the Vallon-Pont-d'Arc. People were swimming in the river under the arch and camping along the river. We asked about camping, paid our fee and yes we had to find a spot for our tent and did, dinner was furnished as was the case in most of the campgrounds we stayed in in Europe.

The next day we were slow to get started, after the climb from the day before. We were in no hurry to tackle another climb. As we started our ride we were surprised to find the route flat to rolling with very little climb, mostly rolling hills. The payback was great with each downhill longer and smoother. As we approached Chamborigaud we could hear a marching band playing and thought how nice it was that we were being welcomed with a marching band. Well, not really, the band was in celebration of WWII and not for us at all. The celebration was great, except, all the hotels were "complete, complete" meaning just that, FULL. We could not find a place to stay in Chamborigaud. We stopped in a produce store to get some fruit and the sales lady became excited, "Americans were in town as they celebrated their liberation by the Americans during WWII."

When we asked about a place to stay, she said, "The butcher's wife had good English and she would call her and she would help us find a place to stay." We kept waiting for the butcher's wife to come and finally decided to walk to a hotel just to see if anyone had cancelled their reservation. As we approached the hotel, we heard a voice behind calling us at the top of her lungs, "monsieur dame" "monsieur dame," and as we looked back, a lady in a wrap-around skirt was running full speed toward us. There were no secrets left, as the skirt was wide open, and looked like Super-man's cape as she ran to catch up with us. This was the butcher's wife. Her English was not much better than my French, which in truth is none, so we attempted to communicate with hands more than voices. But she did have a place for us to stay, she said, "Over the Shell station" and Ann understood "Shell station" and she remembered an abandoned gas station in Montana and began to tell me that she was not going to stay in another gas station. I tried to assure Ann that was not the case. I let the lady know we wanted to stay OVER the Shell station. And then I went too far, I asked, "What is the local cuisine?" "Oh! Monsieur, the pourceau rognon, it is the best in France, and the restaurant on the river has the very best rognon in France. If you would like I will make you a reservation for this evening." "Yes!" "Please make a reservation." At this time Ann was asking me, "What is rognon?" "What is rognon?" Over and over and all I wanted to do was make the butcher's wife happy that she could help us enjoy our stay in Chamborigaud.

After I got Ann calmed down and she understood we would get a room OVER the Shell station and that I would look up rognon when we checked into our room, it appeared all was going well. Until, I checked on pourceau rognon, (swine kidney), not the thing to tell your wife she was having for dinner. "No way!" She screamed, "We used to feed them to our cat, and I am not eating hog kidneys." "Oh! You will not have to, just order poisson, fish, or poulet, chicken, and I will eat the rognon to please the chef."

We honored our reservation. We were seated at a wonderful table, the napkins were placed over our laps with great fanfare and the water was served. Next the very large menus were placed in our laps. The owner stood by as Ann said, "Poisson," he said "No, no madam, rognon." Ann said "No, no poulet," and again he said, "No, no madam rognon." I could tell we were going to have rognon no matter what we wanted to eat, so I said to Ann, "This is a two bottles of wine night and we are going to eat rognon." We ordered the first bottle of wine, and the rognon. Before the order came we had started on the second bottle of wine so by the time the rognon was served it was just fine and the evening ended on a very happy note. The walk back to the Shell station, was a little wobbly but we slept very soundly. The next morning Ann spotted the Viaduct of Chamborigaud, with Mont Lozère in the background. She began to explain about the Roman aqueduct and how the Romans ruled France. Just as she finished the history lesson a train roared across her aqueduct and dispelled her theory about the long bridge over the valley.

    The next morning we ate breakfast in our room and loaded our bicycles to head to Albi, home of Henri Marie Raymond de Toulouse-Lautrec-Monfa, commonly known as Henri Tourlouse-Lautrec. Along the way we met a German bicyclist who told us we would have to ride down the Gorge de Tarn to reach Albi. Down sounded so good but he said nothing about a major mountain pass to get to the Gorge de Tarn. We rode 23 kilometers up to the top of the pass and found a great place to stop for a rest. We watched a group of hikers and their pack animals walk past before we mounted our bicycles and began our ride DOWN the Gorge de Tarn. We continued this great ride down toward Albi, and passed a power plant where the workers gave us a rousing "Bon Voyage." We rode 75 kilometers before reaching the town of Millau. It was late and the clouds had moved in to cover the sky. So we checked into a motel on the trail but outside of town. We walked into town to eat dinner. It looked like rain most of the day but did not come until we were eating. We ordered spaghetti and cheese, that is just what we got spaghetti and cheese, we protested until the waiter came with a small serving of tomato sauce. But the wine was great! The salad was supposed to be an assortment, what that meant was pasta and meat, the dessert was the best, bananas, rum, chocolate and we added ice cream. Remember, I said it started raining after we arrived at the restaurant. We asked the waiter to call a cab so we could return to the hotel. He did, but we waited and waited and asked him if the cab was coming, "Oh yes but he is waiting until the rain stops." So we waited also until the cab finally came and we returned to our hotel.

From Millau we rode down the gorge to the small town of Le Truel and arrived around 1:30 p.m., went into an auberge, where they served breakfast, lunch, dinner and also had rooms for rent. This was at the end of everything. Most of the salad bar was empty. They seated us, and asked if they could serve us lunch, yes, and then they left us sitting alone as the workers from the power plant exited the auberge. After a while they returned with a beautiful salad plate, greens, meats and all the trimmings. We ate and began to wait for the waitress to return to ask in our best French, L'addition, s'il vous plait, or the bill, she never returned until, out of the kitchen came a line of servers with covered plates. Voila! They uncovered the dishes and a very large leg was exposed on each plate, with potatoes and peas. We looked at each other and began to dig into this serving, thinking this was the end, no way! Next came the fromage (cheese) tray, then the dessert tray and we were very well fed. Finally about 3:00 p.m. I was able to ask for the L'addition, s'il vous plait. We thought we would still be able to make Albi before the end of the day, only 10 kms to go and all down river.

Again, not so fast, the owner came out to see our loaded bicycles and asked if we would stay the night. "No we are going to Albi and should be there before dark." "You'll never make it today," "Oh!" "It is only 10 kms and we can make that," he said no more, but as we headed out of town, the wind hit us with such force we almost fell over. I looked at Ann and we decided he was right; we could not make it today. The wind comes up in the afternoon and blows up the Tarn River valley at such force it could stop a train, so we went back, checked in with the owner and spent the night. That evening we walked over to a local store, found a 6 franks bottle of wine, (about $1.00 US) and two glasses from the auberge, climbed up to a wall overlooking the town, drank the wine and wrote our memories of the day's ride.

In 2001, we returned to Le Truel, as we had to cross the Tarn River and picked Le Truel. I sent the owner a letter, photos of our visit and asked for the goose leg but he was unable to get the legs, however we enjoyed our revisit with the friend we had made on our first ride across France.

The next morning the wind was at our backs and the road was downhill as we headed to Albi. Along the way we rode over a very steep pass and found a 4.5 kms unlighted tunnel facing us so we took a detour around that tunnel only to run into another tunnel, also unlit, and about a 1.8 kilometers long. We turned on our lights and hoped for the best, no cars. Just as we exited the tunnel we met our first car and a bicyclist who had been riding our tail lights flew past and gave both of us a shock that anyone else had been in the tunnel with us. We stopped in the shadow of Brousse-le-Chateau an old Castle overlooking the city, and headed down an old country road with little traffic into Albi.

As we were riding into Albi, my chin became like that of Dick Tracy, SQUARE. No pain, just a square chin, Ann asked if something was going on and I said, "Yes, but what it is I do not know." "I do not have a tooth ache, just that my face is swelling." She let me know that as soon as we checked into a hotel, I was going to see a dentist. So after we checked into the Hotel Laperouse, I asked where I could find a dentist.

Next door and up the steps, this I did. Without an appointment, I walked into the dentist's office and the receptionist took one look at my face and ushered me back to an examination room. The dentist was called, he looked at my face, and began to look for rotten teeth. Then he stepped back, put his hands on his hips and said, "SUCRE! SUCRE! SUCRE!" I knew he was saying SUGAR, SUGAR, SUGAR, as I had been eating ever eclair I could find in France, and now something had gone wrong with the salivary glands in my mouth, PLUGGED, yes PLUGGED, so he gave me a prescription, a lecture, in French and sent me out the door, no bill. I found a drug store, filled the prescription, took the medicine and in a couple hours my face began to return to its normal shape.

On our first night in Albi we had duck and our first taste of "fromage blanc" a white cream cheese with a honey mixture and very sweet. This was the best dessert in France, even better than the eclairs I had been eating.

The next day we stopped to explore the Cathedral Basilica of Saint Cecilia also known as Albi Cathedral. It is the most important Catholic building in Albi, and the seat of the Catholic Archbishop of Albi. First built as a fortress in the aftermath of the Albigensian Crusade; begun in 1282 and under construction for 200 years, it is claimed to be the largest brick building in the world, and has frescoes all around the walls and on the ceiling of this massive building. While we were there, we were told of a musical event planned for that evening. The title of the program was the "Tower of Babel." Yes, that was what it was a lot of Babel, I do not know how to describe the music except to say BABEL.

The rain came during the night. We wanted to ride to Toulouse. The more we sat around the more it rained. We decided to ride in the rainy warm day. What would it hurt to get wet. Well after four hours of rain it became a chore to keep going. So we began to look for a place to stay, but each town was complete. We began to look for other routes to other towns and hoped to find a place to stay. We rode eight kms. off route to the town of Lavaur, and still no luck, except there was a train station in Lavaur. We could get out of the rain. I asked the station master if the train ran to Toulouse, and he said, "There is one coming in a few minutes." They will also take your bicycles. We bought tickets for us and the bicycles and went over, sat down, and began to wait for the train. Well it is not that simple, if there are no passengers to catch the train it does not stop. The station master came out, took our tickets and us and walked out on the platform and stuck the tickets into a reader. The arm on the pole flew up and he said the train will now stop. When the train arrived, Ann and I waited until the train car stopped in front of us, it was the last car. We began to load our bicycles, the train master helped us load them on to the car, then he took our tickets and with a frown on his face he said, "You are in the wrong car, you must get in the first car." I began to move the bicycles back to the door, and then he said, "There's no one in the car, sit down." We did but when we arrived in Toulouse it was still raining, even harder. We had not asked if this was an usual thing but later found that it did not rain at that time of year in Toulouse. There was flooding because of all the rain. We also learned that people had been washed down the Garonne River and drowned. We were just lucky we caught the train and lucky that we did not get caught in a flood.

When we departed the train, we could see a sign for a hotel across the street and headed for it. When I asked about a room the desk clerk said there is only one room left and if we took the room it also came with tickets to the Women's World Basketball Championship. What more could we ask for a room, and a world championship to attend. Most of our day had been in the rain, so we walked to the arena and watched France demolish Portugal. We walked a couple blocks where a maitre d' was standing in the door, we asked about a table and yes he could seat us. Then Ann asked, "No fumeˊ (no smoking)," he smiled and brought his hand from behind his back, and took a puff off of his cigarette. We just laughed and followed him to a table. Service was great and after dinner we returned to the tournament to watch Spain and Japan. The ladies from Japan were taller than the Spanish ladies and of course they won the game. Again we walked through the rain back to the hotel. We took the next day off as it was still raining.

    We spent most of the day getting ready to ride if the rain ever stopped. Also we visited the Toulouse Cathedral, which is two churches molded into one. After a day of more basketball and lying around we were tired of the rain and decided we would rent another car and head to Paris. Since we had to get the bicycles and ourselves to the Toulouse Airport to pick up the rental car, we decided to ride. I found what looked like a sure route to the airport but about a mile out of Toulouse, the road ended at the entrance to the A&E, (interstate highway). We were sitting on our bicycles and looking at the map as to how to get to the airport when a policeman rode up on his bicycle and asked if we needed instructions. I explained that we had rented a car at the airport and needed to get the bicycles and ourselves to the airport, "No problem, come with me," and down on the A&E and off to the airport we went. The highway had a wide shoulder but the automobiles and trucks were flying and the wind whipped us around. It was great to see the exit to the airport. Off we went and picked up our rental.

    It was still raining and we were on the south side to the Garonne River and it was flooding. We could not find a bridge across the river as they were closed due to the flooding. We drove west along the river hoping to find a way north. We found a one lane bridge which must have been built during the Roman times as it was sway backed. We had a very uneasy crossing.

They were using red and green lights for the crossing allowing only a few cars on the bridge at a time. Wow! We are across and heading toward Paris. Along the way we stayed at a farm, a castle, and an auberge.

We also decided to do some sight-seeing and drove to the Loire Valley. Our first night in the valley we stayed in an auberge overlooking the Chateau of Chambord. We were surprised, it was empty, no art, no furniture, no nothing, just a very large Chateau. After the tour, we departed for Chenonceau and much the same, but some furnishings and art and also a wonderful garden to explore.

Since I did not want to drive in Paris we settled on Rambouillet just outside of Paris and turned in the car. We stopped at the Le Gare Hotel. They had one room, but only for one night, so we thought ok, we would take the room and since it was conveniently located next to the train station (le Gare) we could take the train to Paris. The next morning the owner who reminded us of Archie Bunker, said we could have the room for one more night, so we went to Paris for the day. The next morning the same thing, one more night, by now it was the weekend and we were thinking we would head out to Chartres to see the Cathedral of Chartres and the beautiful stained glass windows but again the owner said you can have the room for one more night and attend the music festival. What music festival? That was the reason we could have the room for only one night as people attending the festival were canceling their reservations. So we went to the music festival and the first act was an "Elvis Impersonator." We let the stage know we were from Memphis. Elvis came to the table at the break. We offered to buy him a drink, and to our surprise a tray of beers came out of nowhere, free. We were the one's getting as much or more attention than Elvis. Soon a table sent the waiter over and we were asked to join their table. They were from Paris, out to hear the music and enjoy the festival. We felt like royalty!

The next day was Sunday with low traffic in the morning. We rode to Chartres, visited the Cathedral and planned the rest of our ride. We would ride west to join back up to the Loire and then to the coast and back to Amsterdam. Not so fast as we reached Le Lude sur Loire, we realized we were running out of time and needed to head north to Le Mont-Saint-Michel. With some creative map reading we could ride to Saint Susanna then to St James and on to Le Mont-Saint-Michel, a three-day ride that would put us on the Normandy Coast.

As we were approaching Saint Susanna we began to hear a very unfamiliar sound, like an interstate highway, I checked the map, no highways except the one we were riding. The noise would grow to a high pitch and then slowly die down and then began again. We rode to the top of a hill and discovered the source of the noise, guinea fowls, thousands of them. The French refer to them as la pintade. One would start to run and make their noise and all the others would join in. The noise would grow to a high pitch and then they would calm down and it would begin again. That evening in Saint Susanna we had la pintade for dinner, all dark meat.

The next day we headed to St James. What a surprise when we came within sight of the town, a very large American flag flying over the city. We could not believe our eyes but when we entered St. James we discovered the reason, a large U.S. cemetery from WWII. We found a place to stay and discovered it was full of runners, yes runners, why? We did not ask and we did not know what was going to take place the next day. When morning came for us all the runners were gone, at breakfast we were alone.

We loaded our bicycles, and headed to Le Mont-Saint-Michel, just before we came to Le Mont-Saint-Michel, we found a bicycle path and began to ride along with several runners. The crowd was cheering and we were smiling and then we discovered why so many runners. We were leading the winners of the Le Mont-Saint-Michel Marathon to the finish line. We felt like a couple of idiots and speeded on out of the race to the castle of Le Mont-Saint-Michel. The place was empty, so we checked for a room and there would be plenty later in the day. "Do you have security for the bicyclette (bicycles)?" "Oh!" "Yes, we will keep your bags and you will help carry the bicyclettes to the top of the castle and place them on the roof." This we did, rented the room and they in turn stored our panniers.

Sunday morning at Le Mont-Saint-Michel was very quiet, the race was over and only a few runners had stayed at Le Mont-Saint-Michel. There was one group, a group of runners from the USA and their spouses. The day before we had made friends with a waiter and he was pleased to serve us breakfast the next morning. As we were sitting and talking to him the door to the restaurant flew open and in "she" came, the ugly American. "BONJOUR EVERYBODY!" Everyone just looked at her and then again, "BONJOUR EVERYBODY." In a very soft voice, I said to the waiter, please speak only French to us as if we are not from the USA. Please do not let anyone think we are associated in anyway with that person. He did and we had a wonderful omelette aux oeufs, (egg omelet).

From Le Mont-Saint-Michel we rode to the town of Avranches, which is the town General Patton liberated during the Second World War. The traffic was heavy and very close as they passed us on the streets. We found a small road, a "D road" along the coast to the town of Genets.

When we rode into town, I saw a couple men coming out of an auberge, asked if they were open. Just then the window on the second floor opened and the lady of the house stuck her head out and said, "Yes we are open but I am not COOKING!" This was a Monday and on most Mondays everything is closed, so I asked about a place to eat and she sent us to one of two pubs. The first one we entered was full, noisy, and we were overlooked. The second was empty, nice, quiet, with a bartender all alone. I asked if they were serving food, "Maybe" was his answer. So we ordered a glass of wine, and talked to each other until he could not stand to sit by quietly any longer, he said "Anglaise?" "No, les États-Unis d'Amérique, Memphis, Tennessee." When I said that his eyes lit up and he began to dig under his bar for something Ann said, "Elvis," and I said "No, Blues." Blues it was, Muddy Waters, BB King and others, he played the music and we pretended we knew something about the sounds. Lots of smiles and then he said, "Manger le diner" "Oui" and he invited us to eat with his family and we did. This was the second time we had dinner with the family of the owner, first at the auberge in southern France and now in Genets.

We decided to ride along the coast and stopped at a hotel in the town of Port Diélette. We had a window overlooking the sea. We took a day off for the first time in twelve days. This was a lazy day, we walked the beach, watched the tide come in and go out, leaving the boats sitting on the bottom of the harbor. This was a no-star town, with not even a postcard telling anything about the town. It was peaceful, just the right thing for a day off.

The next day we rode 55 kms to Quineville, visited Utah and Omaha Beaches, the museums and gun placements overlooking the English Channel. Then along the Normandy

Beaches, stopping to review the history of each battle. The cemeteries and battles took their toll on a person reading of all the states, religions, and names of so many killed to give us the freedom to ride a bicycle all over the world without fear of harm.

Sunday, July 2, 2000, we were riding east toward Belgium. It was the last day of the European Soccer Championship. France defeated Italy by a score of 2 to 1 and France had exploded into madness. We checked into a small chambre d'hôte, when I asked about security for the bicyclettes the lady said, "Not tonight, you must secure your own bicyclettes, France has won the championship and the country has lost its mind! Put them in your room." France had lost its mind, they even painted their cars red, white and blue, as well as each other. They were riding on top of their cars, flags flying with the noise of horns all night. There were reports of cars being burned in Paris but where we were there was just great joy in winning the European Championship.

Le Mont-Saint-Michel had to be one of our favorite places to have visited, along with the Eiffel Tower, Arc de Triomphe, Louvre Museum, Notre Dame De Paris, Gorges de l'Ardèche, Vallon-Pont-d'Arc, etc. Then there was Honfleur, a harbor town with a small closed harbor surrounded by many shops, cafes and the church of Honfleur which was built by ship builders. The roof is an upside down hull of a boat. There is a large sculpture of a thumb. The room in the auberge was large enough that we could keep our bicycles in our room. It was such a pleasant town that we spent three nights there before riding to the birth place of Joan of Arc, in Rouen. From Rouen, we took a train to Dieppe, back to the English Channel.

With a great tailwind we rode 60 kms in less than four hours to reach St Valery Sur Somme. This was another town to fall in love with, as our room overlooked the large salt marsh where the tide had rolled in and out. That evening we ate dinner in a family setting, everyone wanted to know where we had visited in France and how we had enjoyed our trip by bicycle. They, like so many, could hardly believe we had traveled so far on a bicycle, even in a country where we thought everybody enjoyed bicycling.

The next day we rode 70 kms near Villiers where we discovered a chambre d'hôte and a wonderful landlady, Madam Boschin with a constant companion, a Bichon named Domino, pure white dog with two black eyes. Her greatest concern was, "Are you going to visit Le Touquet?" "No the traffic is heavy and we are getting close to returning to Amsterdam." "We are going to pass Le Touquet." "Not So!" Madam Boschin drove us along with domino into Le Touquet. She let us out where the street became one way into town and said she would pick us up where the one-way street exited the town. We walked to the beach, found a place to eat, and had our first taste of quinoa, a grain, but this was very bland. We met three people from England, Henry, Doug and Rosemary. They had taken the Chunnel over, with their car, just to take Henry out to dinner in a town he had helped liberate during WWII. Henry looked the part of a tall British military officer, tall and very handsome! They were surprised we had traveled so far on our bicycles and we were surprised they had come over for the evening through the Chunnel. When we finished dinner and our sight-seeing in Le Touquet, we called Madam Boschin and met her on the edge of town.

The next day, July 12, we decided we would head cross country to Belgium. I had found the listing of an auberge in the country. Late that afternoon around 7:00 p.m., we finally found the auberge, no rooms just a place for breakfast, lunch, and dinner, after riding all day we almost dropped right there in the court yard. But as luck has always been on our side, it was again today. The owner knew where there was an auberge in Sains-lès-Fressin, 8 kms away. It was after 7:00 p.m. and the chance of riding 8 kms before dark, really dark, was out of the question. I asked if we could camp in her barn, she smiled and said "Oh!" "My husband will drive you and your bicycles to Sains-lès-Fressin to the auberge." He pulled up in a Fiat pick-up truck and motioned for me to load the bicycles into the truck. I attempted to place one bicycle in the truck, no way. I unloaded our panniers, laid them in the bed of the truck. Then the bicycles on top of the panniers with them hanging out of the truck. Then the three of us were off to Sains-lès-Fressin.

The next day we continued to Belgium. About noon we met a man in Alquines and asked about a place to eat. He motioned left, la gauche, then straight, tout droit, (when I asked for directions in France the first words were always, tout droit, straight ahead) I asked how far? He motioned stay, then he came back with his wife, and she said, tout droit, la gauche, (straight ahead, left) and motioned around the corner, as we rounded the corner, there was the restaurant. After lunch we headed to Ardres, the first reservation we had. The Chambre-d-hotl was beautiful. With a pond in the middle of the square loaded with fish, and flowers everywhere.

We would spend another night in France, right on the border of France and Belgium, in the "Hotel Terimus." The place looked like a bordello, (Maison de prostitution) and we passed it several times before we decided that it was the only place to stay. Our room was total royal purple and looked like the insides of a French whore house, but since I had never been in a French whore house, I could only guess, and so would Ann as she made that statement several times while we were in the room. The place was clean, and the landlady was great, really out of the past as she was dressed in a long gown with feathers and furs. We would laugh about this place for a long time.

With sadness we left France after a little over two months of touring through the French countryside. It had really been a wonderful experience even without enough language for good communication except by sign language. But our vacation was getting short and we must head across Belgium and back to the Netherlands.

As we headed east across Belgium, our stay would take us to Bruges for a much-needed rest and a few days off to explore the city. We arrived on a Saturday and most of the hotels are complete (no rooms), so off to the VVV for help. They helped, a four-star hotel, a suite, and a price tag large enough to set us back to tent camping. The second night the hotel helped us out and moved us into a regular room for the rest of our stay. We did all the tourist things, museums, churches, and the boat rides through the city. It took most of the day on Tuesday to find our way out of the city.

We discovered a wonderful bicycle path heading toward the Netherlands but with one slowing factor, rabbits, and pheasants, they would appear out of no-where and run across the bicycle path. We had to dodge them or worse, kill a poor animal or bird. Oh! Yes, there were examples of that happening as we saw many of them that had been killed by bicyclists.

As we rode along I noticed a large group of bicyclists riding a distance behind us and slowly gaining on Ann and me. Suddenly, one of the riders broke from the group and sprinted to catch us. As he approached he shouted, "Guten Tag!" I said "Good day to you" in English, "He almost lost control of his bicycle and said "You are Americans."

"Yes" "We thought you were from Germany because you are wearing helmets." "No, Americans." Then he said in amazement, "You are touring on touring bicycles." "Yes," "Where have you been and where are you heading?" "We have been touring from Amsterdam to the south of France and now heading back to Amsterdam." "Will you stop long enough to have a beer with us because we would love to hear your story?" "Sure, we will do anything for a beer." They all stopped at a local hang-out and we drank a beer, talked about our trip, and enjoyed getting to know a large group of retired Eastman Kodak employees.

Sometimes you get good advice along the way and sometimes you get bad advice. One of the men began to tell us about a great place to stay in Dendermonde. So let me set the stage in another light, the hotel he recommended, had a bocce court under the front windows of the rooms in the front of the building, also those windows are the only ones with a view, and they have to be opened in late July to cool the rooms. A bocce game is very loud and they last into the night. We had ridden 15 kms off course to get to Dendermone, so really 30 kms out of the way and felt we had been sent to hell instead of a good place to visit.

We were getting closer and closer to the end of a wonderful tour through the Netherlands, Belgium and France. We rode into Westmalle, Belgium and stopped to buy a picnic lunch. We sat on a bench deciding how to leave town, we spotted a bicycle path in the direction we needed to travel. Also we were watching gliders overhead and marveled at the number in the sky. As we rode along, the gliders faded away and we came to a point in the trail to go right or left so we picked left as that appeared to be the correct direction toward the Netherlands. In a short time we noticed more gliders flying and again marveled at the number of gliders. Then reality set in as we realized we were back in Westmalle. We had made a circle and ended up back where we had bought our lunch. We ate lunch on the bench where we found the bike path which went in a circle. We started the day 15 kms off the route and now we had lost another 16 kms. Over all we rode 60 kms with 31 kms in lost time.

When we arrived in Brecht, we went to the VVV to find a room, the young man asked if we wanted to stay in a youth hostel, no we were too old to do that, what else? There was a farm outside town for the elders, how about there? Great, that will work, so we stayed on a farm, with, 24 horses, 2,000 chickens, a large number of ducks and geese, 2 parrots, and 4 deer. Of course Ann was in animal heaven as there were pets of each species.

From Brecht we rode hard for two days into Breda, Netherlands. As we rode into town we spotted an outdoor restaurant and pub, so we stopped for a beer, Ann likes light colored beer and I like my beer, the darker the better. She ordered her beer by asking the waiter, I ordered my beer by the name because it had Dunkel, (dark) attached to the name. I drank my beer before Ann and felt a real buzz and ordered another beer, with a different name but with Dunkel attached to the name. The waiter said, "Sir, I must warn you, this is a much stronger beer than the first one you ordered." "How much stronger?" "This one has alcohol in it." "You mean you let me order a non-alcohol beer?" "Sir, I thought you knew what you were doing." We had a great laugh and I still enjoy telling about the waiter and his response when I found out I had a non-alcohol beer.

With only a few days before we have to return home, we set out for Haarlem, thought we could make it but just ran out of time. We arrived in Nieuwkoop, a resort town on a lake with a wonderful inn for the night, great food, funny waitresses, dressed in red pepper pants, (like those peppers from Tabasco), and lots of jokes, and enjoyment for the evening. The next day we reached Haarlem and packed to return to the USA. Over a 72-day period we covered three countries, 1,000's kms, visited the most wonderful places, and met the greatest people. We were looking forward to 2001 to return for another bicycle ride in Europe.

Bicycling Ireland 2001
(using two books listed below)

"Ireland by Bike"
SECOND EDITION
by: Robin Krause
21 Tours Geared for Discovery
Tours number: 1, 2, 3, 4, 5, 6, 12, 13, 14, repeat, 14. 13, 12, then number 10 and 7 ending in Cork
Part I: **"France by Bike"**
Part II: "14 Tours Geared for Discovery"
by: Karen and Terry Whitehill
A list of Tours in the order we rode them in 2001: Tour No. 1, Tour No. 2, Tour No. 3, Tour No. 6, Tour No. 7, and Tour No. 8

This vacation was to begin on May 20, 2001, but a rain storm hit the Memphis Airport and our flight was canceled, the Airport stored our bicycles and panniers overnight and we departed a day later for Dublin. On May 22, we arrived in the Dublin Airport and found our reservations at the B&B in Sword, north of the airport, had been given to a "regular" but she had another place we could stay. This B&B was located in Malahide. Upon arriving at the B&B our landlady would not let us bed down but sent us into Dublin for the day to get our clocks set to Ireland time. On the ride into Dublin, the traffic was bumper to bumper and no bicycle lane. That night I worried as to how we would get through Dublin and then a great brain wave hit! Take the train from Malahide to Dun Laoghaire and miss the Dublin traffic. The next day we rode to the train station in Malahide, bought two passenger tickets and two bicycle passes. When DART arrived we loaded the bikes and ourselves and off to Dun Laoghaire.

Oh! Not so fast, as we approached the center of Dublin, and more people loaded on the train, they began to push our bicycles out of their way, and complained as to why bicycles were on DART. When we reached Connolly Station, a station master spotted us and our bicycles on DART. He pushed the doors open, held them open and asked, why we were on DART with bicycles. "We have our tickets and bicycle passes and we are heading to Dun Laoghaire." "No you are not you cannot be on DART with bicycles." "Sir, the traffic in Dublin is impossible to ride in and we just lack a little more to reach Dun Laoghaire, please let us stay on the train." Even the passengers on DART began to chant, "Give them a break, give them a break," but he was unmoved by our complaint or protests from the other passengers. He said, "You cannot be on DART with bicycles." He motioned for two workers to come over and take our bicycles down, and informed them to get our money and pay us back, then he asked, "Where did you get those tickets?" "Malahide" "Heads will roll over this." Then Ann stepped up as we exited the train, shaking her finger in his face and said, "If we get killed in Dublin, our blood will be on your hands." With a great big Irish smile he said, "Lady come back and haunt me."

When we exited Connolly Station, there was a bicycle lane on the street and we soon found a bicycle path all the way to Dun Laoghaire. Our blood is not on his hands and he did us a favor by putting us off, and giving us our money back, a free ride into Dublin.

We soon discovered our reservations in Dun Laoghaire were changed, much as in Sword. The landlady informed us the plumbing was broken and she had made arraignments for us to move to another B&B. The new B&B was Tara B&B, just down the street a couple blocks not like we had when changing from Sword to Malahide. The new landlady informed us the original B&B had over booked and it was not bad plumbing. We stayed two nights in Dun Laoghaire, visited Dublin again and also the James Joyce Tower, where he wrote "Ulysses." Our next destination was Wicklow.

In Wicklow we were expecting to stay at the Arches B&B, not so, they informed us our reservations were for the next night and we were a day early. "No, your paper work is incorrect and we are to stay here tonight." The landlady found us a room. The inn keeping seemed very confused in Ireland.

We arrived in St. Brigid, we are really surprised, as we were expected. All was great, the breakfast was eggs, sunny side, roasted tomatoes, porridge, and bread. We had plenty of fuel to ride to Shillelagh for lunch and on to Kilkenny, a 65 mile trip. The next day we took the train to visit the Waterford Crystal factory in Waterford. When we returned to Kilkenny it was dinner time and we found the Toulouse-Lautrec Brasseurs. We started with mussels, then duck, a bottle of wine, and apple and plum crunch with ice cream, and a lot of history of Ireland by the owners.

During the next week we rode to Cashel, Tipperary, Limerick Lahinch, Doolin, along the Cliffs of Moher, to Galway. We were staying at the Rock Haven B&B. The landlady met us in the back yard with our bicycles, showed us where to store the bikes, and made us enter her establishment properly, through the front door, where she met us with tea, served perfectly. If you have ever watched, "Keeping up Appearances" the landlady could be the lady in the show, everything must be perfect, prim, and proper. We took a day off in Galway and visited the aquarium and a live show that evening.

As we had reservations in Doolin and a fifty-mile ride, oh, yes it was raining. Breakfast was porridge, but as we are fixing the porridge, the landlady informed us the traditional way to eat good Irish porridge was with a wee bit of good Irish Whiskey, "Would you like a wee smidge on your porridge?" "Oh, yes," and she began to pore the whiskey on the porridge, stop, stop, we have fifty miles to ride today, "Don't worry the rain will keep you going as well as the good Irish whiskey." I suppose it did as we made the fifty miles and arrived at our B&B and received a welcome like you would never expect when you are soaking wet. The landlady took our wet rain suits, our shoes, and all the wet things and dried everything. The next morning, even our shoes were toasty dry. They had been in the furnace room.

We rolled along through the countryside, took a ferry and ended in Trelee without a reservation. We made several calls to find a B&B, found one, showered, napped, and began to search for tickets to the National Theater, to attend a live production of songs and dances.

Again, rain as we left Trelee, we found a garage to hide in about 10 kms outside of town and sat out most of the rain. Later we found a pub for lunch. A surprise, The South Pole. The original owner was Tom Crean, the Boatswain's Mate for Captain Shackelford of The Endurance. Ann and I had just finished reading a book about the Endurance. So we spent a lot of time talking to the people in the pub. We reached Dingle that afternoon and had a disappointing dining experience with a very rude owner and walked back to the B&B in a bad mood. We had just spent more for dinner than our lodging and the evening came up short.

The Dingle Peninsula, was truly the best part of our ride in Ireland. The Slea Head Loop on the Dingle Peninsula was the best of the best for bicycling in Ireland. This ride took us along the Atlantic Ocean and into Inch for lunch. Inch is a long stretch of beach where a USA bomber landed during WW II and the people of Inch gave them a warm welcome. From Inch it was downhill all the way to Killarney. We rode miles in the rain, before stopping for the night. With all the rain we decided to skip Bantry Bay, this is where my ancestors, The White's, are from. Also the Earl of Bantry is a White and had promised to welcome us with a tune on his Sax, but with the rain coming everyday in buckets, we skipped Bantry Bay and headed on toward Cork.

The next day we rode 55 more miles to reach a farm B&B just outside Cork. We took the bus into Cork each day and enjoyed the farm each afternoon. The owners had a young son who wanted to teach me "hurling" a kind of ball and bat game where the players carry scars from being hit across the face by their opponent. In the evening we would walk to Murphy's Pub for dinner each night. The owners of Murphy's were a set of twins, Brandon and Brad Coleman and played on the "All County Cork" all Ireland Championship in 1976. One afternoon the landlady let us know not to be afraid on our way home as the street would be full of men, they would be "Road Bowling." This is a game of rolling a two-pound steel ball down the road, around curves, and distance counts. We were warned to stand with the men as the ball can break a leg if you are hit with it. We did as they said. When the ball would roll off the road in the dark, they always found it quickly and it would start all over again. I asked the landlady how they could find the ball so quickly? "Oh!" "That is simple, they use a metal detector." Easy enough.

We had had enough rain and decided to head to France. We caught a ferry from Ringaskiddy (near Cork) to Roscoff, France. This was a 17-hour ferry ride across the English Channel. We arrived in France on Sunday June 17, 2001.

France by Bicycle for the second time!

"France by Bicycle"
by Karen and Terry Whitehill

We took two days off in Roscoff before heading to Brest. Brest was the headquarters for the U-boats during WW II. Now it is the headquarters of the French submarine service. Also Brest has one of the most interesting aquariums in the world. We found a place to stay near the aquarium and spent the next day touring the different oceans and fish from around the world. As we watched a film about the South Pole, across the bottom of the film they showed the Emperor Penguins and as the screen for the film began to rise up, there stood real Emperor Penguins along the glass in the aquarium. There were three distinct areas in the aquarium, the Atlantic Shelf, the Tropics and the third was the North/South poles.

We had done our homework and found a foot ferry across the Bay of Brest, going south. The next morning I called and they explained where to catch the ferry. As we rode into town, standing in the middle of the street were the workers for the ferry, waving us to hurry and as soon as they loaded our bicycles and we were aboard, they were off across the bay.

Remember, I told you about the French submarines, well, as we crossed the Bay of Brest, one of France's Nuclear subs was returning to port. Standing on deck was the crew, dressed in bright red uniforms. I was reminded of my time in the US

Navy when we would return to port as we stood at attention while sailing into Newport Harbor in Rhode Island.

When we reached Le Fret, there were two busses with senior citizens hurrying off the busses to load the ferry for Brest. That was the reason on the Brest side for us to hurry along as they needed to pick up the "old folks." The people were amazed at our age, traveling by bicycle. From Le Fret, we rode to Concarneau, along the way we passed through Quimper, and again encountered a group of senior citizens eating lunch, as a group, in the local park. One of the men in the group was so impressed by us that he found a bottle of wine and cups and invited us to share a toast for riding across France That evening we checked into the Hotel French, in Concarneau and met our first American, she was from Canada and again very impressed that we were traveling by bicycle. She told us about an area south where the ladies wore the most beautiful lace hats and bonnets, so we detoured off our map but did not discover any of the ladies.

Wednesday, we rode from Concarneau to Quimperlé and stopped in the tourist office to find a place to stay, while we were waiting our turn, I noticed a poster advertising a music festival that night. We discovered it would be a festival of music and dance recitals of the classes from all the schools in Quimperlé. This turned into a night of joy and fun as we walked around Quimperlé from one location to another on the streets of Quimperlé. One of the first recitals we encountered consisted of five harpists. One harpist was a very young girl who entertained everyone with her tongue. For every note she played on the harp, she changed the location of her tongue, from one side of her lips to the other, always sticking it out of her mouth. There were dancers in dresses flowing in the wind, and ballet dancers too. We walked all around town, ending the evening at the town square where a mixed group of musical instruments was played by the young and old, then more dancers, and at last the choral groups. This was truly a local affair as the people who walked around town knew each other and the performers.

We left Quimperlé on Friday and rode to the Le Bretagne Hotel outside the small town of Regnic. We had ridden 80 kms. As we arrived, a wedding party also arrived for their reception. The father of the groom spotted us, introduced us to M/M Raymond, had us stand with the lucky couple for photos, and gave us an invitation to attend the reception. Our host insisted we speak French, and began to give us a lesson in French, by the end of the evening we were mumbling through a few French phrases and enjoying the beer. The wedding party loaded into cars to caravan around the town. We stayed behind and drank their beer. When they returned the cars were decorated in all sorts of designs, all with eye lashes over the head lights.

Saturday, June 24, 2001, became a red-letter day! We entered the town of Guer in the middle of the Fete-du-Cheval (The Festival of Horses). We were able to get a room and enjoy the festival. That night we bought tickets to a musical and dance and attended thinking we would just watch, not so! As we sat along the wall, two men came over and took Ann out on the dance floor. As I laughed about her having to dance two ladies came out of nowhere and took me out to dance. This was a line dance and easy to catch on to so we enjoyed the evening as we danced the night away, and laughed with the locals.

Sunday morning the Fete-du-Cheval was still going on with a parade of old cars and vintage bicycles. The bicycles were decorated with flowers and corn stalks and the riders dressed in country overalls, much like the farmers of the USA.

We did not stay for all the festival on Sunday but headed out in the middle of the parade. We decided to ride hard, stop and picnic. This we did at Port de Guipry along the Vilaine River. We watched a river barge navigate through the locks and a fisherman troll along the shore line of the Vilaine. After the picnic, we decided to ride D 772, a yellow road.

I suppose I should have explained earlier that all roads lead to Paris and all the D roads are colored yellow on the Michelin maps. They are less traveled by automobiles. The A&E roads are the interstate type highways, and N roads are very busy and not for bicycle travel. Well that is the highway system 101, there are other roads to stay off of, and roads to ride such as the C roads which are very rural.

Now back to our choice of D 772, as it is a straight shot to Angers which is our destination. We rode hard and fast, as we entered Bain-de-Bretagne, we hit a detour. With the help of several locals directing us, we reached Teillay. Ann needed water so we stopped at a local "le salon," (bar). Here was another one of those times we brought the French to laughter to the point of tears. If anyone owned a camel-back water system in 2001, they will remember it had a water bag that fit inside the liner of the back pack, it had a hose to drink from much as the ones of today, except the water bag had to be taken from the back pack to be filled. I asked the bar tender for his help in filling the bag with ice and water and he agreed. When I pulled the water bag out of the back pack, in unison the ladies said, "douche-bag," and the laughter began. When Ann tested the water, the whole place came apart laughing. We became a part of the crowd and laughed too.

We departed Teillary with the whole bar crowd standing in the street waving us on toward Angers. We finished the detour and returned to D 772 and it began to appear that we would have to beg for a place to stay. We rode 20 kms without seeing anything but farms and then, we rode into Chateaubriant. What a find, a medieval town with a hotel with three (3) stars, the Château de Châteaubriant.

On Monday we rode hard in an attempt to reach Angers. The weather was hot, and the distance continued to stretch out before us. We found a small village on the Loire River outside of Angers, where three rivers come together, the lesser join the Loire. The town's people had turned out in large groups to swim in one of the smaller streams. We thought about joining them but after 90 kms in 100-degree heat, we chose to come back the next day for our swim. Most of the day we rode through fields of corn, wheat, grass, cattle and several horse farms. D 772 ran through a rural area without much in the way of traffic with no towns between Châteaubriant and Angers, the best kind of bicycling.

The Mayenne, the Sarthe, and the Loir, all come from the north and flow south into the Loire River. They meet in Angers. We stopped short of the town of Angers, where we found a Farm Auberge. We ate our meals under the trees in the back of the farm house. The best swimming hole was in the Sarthe as it was shallow with flowing cold water over anyone who lay on the shallow bottom of the river. The bottom of the river had small rocks rolled smooth over the years in the stream.

From the auberge in Rockfort-s-Loire we took a bus into Angers to visit the Black Castle, explored the city on a tour train and spent two or three hours trying to catch a bus back to Rockfort-s-Loire. We left Rockfort-s-Loire on Wednesday heading south to Saumur. We have a saying to each other, "grab a bird in the hand" this is for great places to stop. We passed such a place as we continued down the Loire to Saumur. We passed a beautiful restaurant overlooking the river and 4 kms later we were kicking ourselves as we rode into a truck stop for lunch. At the truck stop, Ann ordered the steak and I ordered the rognons de porc, another mistake, for I had forgotten what rognons de porc were, hog kidneys, a very poor choice for lunch. As we sat in the truck stop a couple from California walked in and we began a conversation which would last for two hours. We compared our travels in France. When we finished lunch and a long conversation with Steve and Heather we rode to the champignon caves (mushroom caves). We discovered many mushrooms we could eat and also a lot we could not eat, especially the red mushrooms, for they are the most poisonous of the mushroom family. I had discovered this in California in 1985 while hiking the PCT, when I found the "snow rose" a beautiful mushroom in the Sierra Mts. of California but very poisonous. After the tour of the mushroom caves we again headed to Saumur. We checked into a nondescript hotel in Saumur and enjoyed pizza for dinner.

After touring the Chateau Saumur, a chateau built in the 16th century, we again headed south with no destination in mind except to ride south. Along the route we found the L'abbaye'fontevraud in Fonlevraud, built 900 years ago, I suppose 920 years ago now since it has been 20 years since we adventured across France. Ann had read the book "Eleanor of Aquitaine" and wanted to visit the L'abbaye'fontevraud, where King Richard the Lion Hearted, his mother, Eleanor of Aquitaine, her husband, King Henry II of England, and a maiden, not Richard's wife are entombed. We were the only visitors and our guide gave us a complete history of the L'abbaye'fontevraud.

We found a farm auberge near Chinon, Auberge de l'Ile, L'Île-Bouchard, one of our best finds in France. The food was great and it was a wonderful place to rest after a long day in the sun. From the auberge, we began our climb out of the Loire valley. This took us along two rivers, the Creuse and the

Vienne Rivers. We entered Descartes where there were five medieval ruins but no place to stay, so we pushed on to La Roche-Posay. As we rode into town we found the town square full of senior citizens playing a bowling game with each player having three steel balls weighing two pounds and a smaller ball which was tossed first and then the other players in that court would attempt to roll their balls closer to the smaller ball. The toss was underhanded in an attempt to have the ball stop close to the smaller ball. The laugh came when we discovered one player, a little old lady with a magnet on a string, using it to pick up her balls.

We liked the looks of the town and the excitement of the day so we decided to check into the Les Loges du Parc Hotel, the most expensive night to date on this ride. Great room, wonderful dinner and we expected a great sleep, but late in the night we were awakened by a motor-scooter racing around the town square, even with the window closed it took quite a while to return to sleep.

Saturday morning we started our ride along the Gartempe River out of La Roche-Posay, and entered the town of Angles-le-S-L'Anglin, a beautiful town getting ready for a festival with the streets full of people. We brought laughter with us as we rode into town, the people were lining the street for a parade. As we approached the crowd we both lost our chain rings. They dropped off the bicycles. We had to walk up a very short climb to the top of the street, with a lot of cat calls from the crowd and laughter for our blunder as we approached the judging stands for the parade.

We finally made it through town and headed to St. Savin and stopped in Antigny for lunch, another outdoor setting in a garden. We were doing a lot of this, this year, but thoroughly enjoyed these lunches. After lunch we walked to 12th century church with beautiful frescos painted in a sepia tone, what a find! From here we rode to Chatellcrault for the night. Our hotel is across the river from the 900-year-old city. Another great find, with a view of the city as we ate dinner and breakfast in another garden setting.

On Sunday we decided to by-pass Poitiers and head to Melle, 83 kms through gently rolling farm land another wonderful place to bicycle with easy riding. As we rode into the town of Ceaux-en-Coule we needed the public rest-room, in France known as the WC (va-say) or water closet. We flagged down a car at a stop sign and began to ask for the WC, the driver said, "Speak English, I am the local English teacher." We had a laugh and asked for the rest-rooms. Then we talked a while as he wanted to know where we were from and what had brought us to Ceaux-en-Coule. We explained we were touring France and just happened to ride through Ceaux-en-Coule on our way to Bordeaux.

Then he directed us into town where we found the usual, "foot-plant rest-room." We left Ceaux-en-Coule for Melle and arrived around 3 p.m. with time to wash clothes but did not make a reservation for dinner. When we arrived at the only restaurant in town it was complete (full) so we begged for sandwiches and a bottle of wine and had a picnic in the town square. This was one of those evenings when a man and his wife enjoy each other to the fullest. I love Ann so very much and pray often that my life will never change as she is truly my love for life.

On Monday we returned to "France by Bicycle," the book we have used for two years as we traveled in France. We followed the route from Melle to Saintes with lots of stops along the way. I think we saw all the churches in between the two towns, as well as a side trip to a cemetery to see the Lantern-of-Death. This is a tall tower with a small hole in the top for a light to guide people to the cemetery.

At lunch time we stopped in Aulnay and the welcome was a laugh, as we stopped at a local tavern, a group of men began to chug-a-lug their drinks to give us their table. They were locals that had emigrated from England. At one church, built in the 12th century the artist had carved elephants with toe nails and frescoes of other animals.

Our ride took us through St. Jean-d-Angely and a struggle with traffic and trouble finding the WC. The temperature had climbed to over 100°s as we reached our destination for the day, Saintes. It was market day and the streets were full of venders and traffic jams but we found a wonderful hotel for the night.

With the heat and a great place to rest we took the day off and decided to board the train into Bordeaux. We visited a beautiful Cathedral, many fountains, statues and a wonderful garden but by the afternoon we were lost. We stood at a bus stop and asked the driver which bus to catch to the La-Gare. He said get on, I attempted to pay, he put his hand over the pay slot, and soon he stopped, pointed to another bus stop, and said catch either number 7 or 8 to the La-Gare. We have found so many wonderful people in France that we understand why the English have emigrated to France.

After a day off to visit Bordeaux we woke up to rain, lots of rain. Since we arrived in Ireland in May and brought a lot of warm clothing but now are in southern France, we packed all the unnecessary clothing and shipped it home just to kill the morning waiting for the rain to stop. We rode south to Bougneau and found a truck stop, hotel, restaurant and decided to stop for the day. A good choice, nice hotel and quiet as we had the place to ourselves.

We continued south the next day to Coutras, a distance of 87 kms.. We arrived around 3 p.m., and found a chambre d'hôte just about 1 km from town. Around 7 p.m. it had quit raining and we walked into town for dinner, salad, escargot, pizza and a banana split and we waddled back to the chambre d'hôte. In case you do not know what a chambre d'hôte is, it is a guest room in a home and this one was a wonderful find.

Friday morning we met our host and hostess for le-petit dejeuner, (breakfast) and we were told we had slept in a home built in 1350. Our host also showed us through the house and pointed out objects from his grandfather and father. He even had his father's bicycle bought in 1935. We had a hard time deciding to leave as it was threatening rain, again.

After much discussion, we headed out in spite of the threat of rain. Along the way it began to thunder and lightning and since we were riding steel frame bicycles, we began to look for a hiding place. The porch of a house, anything, we knocked on a strangers door and two ladies appeared, and yes take your bicycles to the garage. We did and as we stood waiting for the storm to pass, the ladies brought us coffee and cookies. We were fussed over and she asked us to write her a card when we returned to the USA. We really stayed too long, we had so little French and they had no English but we laughed using hand signs to communicate.

That evening we had reached the town of Abzac and found a hotel, it looked closed but after much exploring we spotted a lady at the bar, we stood at a window and motioned how to get inside, she motioned, look down, we did and there was a door knob. We turned the knob and went inside. The two of us were laughing at ourselves when two men walked in behind us. They had watched our mistakes and our laughing at or mistakes, and said, "You must be from the USA, the British do not have a sense of humor and would not be as happy about the door knob." "Yes, we are from Tennessee, USA." We invited the men to join us for lunch and since they had good English, we were able to discuss a lot of the places we had traveled and were planning to travel in the next weeks. When we mentioned riding to Saint-Emillion, they both kissed the ends of their fingers and said "the best vin in France." Also the mention of Figeac brought out the discussion of riding the Cele River, a must according to these men.

When we arrived in Saint-Emillion the next day, it just so happened to be the first day of the Tour-de-France and the town was celebrating the beginning with a bicycle tour of its own. The street ahead of us was full of bicycles, first the club riders, the family riders and then those on antique bicycles. We joined in with the last group through town. Since Saint-Emillion was complete, we decided to continue our ride along the Dordogne. The Dordogne was flooding, and as the road we were riding on was along the shore of the river, we watched the flood waters wash by with lots of trash floating in the river. We came to a fork in the road, a bridge across the river and a road up the side of a mountain. We continued on the road ahead and shortly we came to a sign, lying down which stated "Road Closed" surely not to bicycles, then we came to a fence across the road, we could go around the end of the fence, and we did, then we came to a pile of dirt across the road, and we pushed our bicycles over the dirt pile and continued on the road, now the road had larger cracks in the pavement and appeared to be sliding into the river. We continued and did not have to climb the mountain, then it stopped us, because across the road was a tree with red flashing lights. Ann said, "Roscoe," "I do not think the French will take responsibility for our deaths if we continue on this road." We turned around, went back to the fork in the road, crossed the river on the bridge, and found a safe road on the north side of the river. We found a campground in St. Antoine-de-Breuilh, and rented our first caravan to sleep in for the night.

We continued our trip up the Dordogne and were surprised by the number of people out to check on the river. Large groups of runners, hikers, bicyclists and just locals all taking a look at the river. We stopped in Lalinde, and found a century old hotel, hanging over the river. There were only eight rooms in the hotel, lucky for us, we got one of the rooms, and dinner was on a balcony overhanging the river, where we had the best lamb in France.

On Sunday and Monday we continued along the Dordogne and watched the people cleaning up from the flooding. There was lots of mud and damage from the flood. Ann had seen the map and decided we should ride on to Domme, not on to Domme, up to Domme. It is on the top of a mountain overlooking the Dordogne Valley. A great place to stop but the climb was spoken about that evening by a group of teenage Americans who arrived after we had reached their hotel. The owner mistook us for part of their group, put us in a room and stored our bicycles in the basement of the hotel. The teenagers were discussing how difficult it was to ride up to Domme. We were pleased to let them know we rode the same road on loaded bicycles, while theirs were empty and their gear was in a van.

From Domme we rode to the town of Rocamadour, and checked into the Panorama Hotel overlooking the city. The Cathedral in Rocamadour is carved out of the side of the mountain. We went to see the Cathedral, discovered that evening a choir from the USA was singing, and we attended the concert. That evening in our hotel we discussed passing up the ride to Cabrerets, but we were so pleased that we did not pass this town. Located on the Cele River the auberge was a wonderful find, as the owner made us speak French, and directed us to climb up to the cave, Pech Merle. We made reservations for a tour the next day, and bought our tickets.

We discovered the auberge we were staying in was one of the best in France, five stars.

Pech Merle is a cave which opens into a hillside at Cabrerets in the Occitania region in France. It is one of the few prehistoric cave painting sites in France that remain open to the general public. Extending for over a kilometer and a half from the entrance are caverns, the walls of which are painted with dramatic murals dating from the Gravettian culture (some 25,000 years BC). Some of the paintings and engravings, however, may date from the later Magdalenian era (16,000 years BC). The walls of seven of the chambers at Pech Merle have fresh, lifelike images of woolly mammoth, spotted horses, single colored horses, bovines, reindeer, handprints, and some humans. Footprints of children, are preserved in what was once clay, and they have been found more than half a mile underground. Thanks to the owner we were able to tour the cave. With such a host, how could we leave, so we stayed another day, and enjoyed our landlord. We thought he had a lot more English than he pretended, as his English improved the longer we stayed.

Even with a late start we were in Figeac by 3 p.m., found a room and discovered Figeac was one of the pilgrimage stops across France to Spain. The ride along the river was mostly flat but along very high cliffs, and dropped straight down into the river. Since we were on the north shore and traveling east, we rode along the cliffs bordering the river. Oh! Yes there were a few guard rails but there were also gaps in the guard rails. This type of ride always brings out a lot of worry from Ann. Also there are a lot of tunnels to ride through, although they were short enough to see the other end and we were able to avoid meeting or being passed by an automobile.

In Figeac we met a couple from the Netherlands, traveling by bicycle with their children. We recommended the caves at

Pech Merle as well as the auberge we had stayed in while in Cabrerets. We split a pizza with Dutch couple hiking the pilgrimage trail across France to Spain.

July 14, 2001, Bastille Day! This is a national holiday, it was also a Saturday, and everything was closed. We left Figeac and found our route along the Diego River with lots of climbs, the longest and steadiest climb of our trip. We climbed 7 kms. to the medieval town of Peyrusse-le-Roc for lunch before starting another climb out of the river canyon through tunnels and a rain forest. We found a two (2) star hotel, the Hotel Marre, to end Bastille Day celebrations with the locals.

Sunday is always a great day in France to find a noon meal, and of course the meal is served late in the afternoon which made it possible to arrive in Baraqueville late that afternoon and still get in in time to eat the noon meal. We checked into the De-L'Agricultural Hotel which was a one-star hotel and cheaper than any we had found in France, F185 or $26.45 per night. We were now in the Midi-Pyrénées. We had been climbing all day and looking forward to the usual five course meal. We started with soup, salad, quail, cheese and dessert and oh yes a bottle of very fine wine. We were pampered even in a one-star hotel.

Monday we were looking forward to returning to Le Truel, and staying in the same auberge that we had stayed in 2000. With a translator on my computer I had written to the owner of the auberge and asked if we could give him a day's notice that we were coming, "Would it be possible to stay in his auberge?" "Yes!" I had also made a collage of photos taken when we were in Le Truel and I had enclosed it with the letter. He was very pleased we had remembered him and his wife. There were two major river valleys to cross between Baraqueville and Le Truel, first was the Aveyron River Valley and then a drop of 9 kms. into the Tarn River valley at Le

Truel. On our way down into the valley we had to take it very easy as there was a lot of loose gravel on the road and along the way I had our third flat tire. I attempted to patch the tube, and then had to stop a few kms. later to change the tube in the tire. We arrived in Le Truel late, checked in with much fanfair and readied ourselves for dinner. When we arrived in the dining room, the owner had the photo collage mounted on a board and was taking it from table to table to show everyone his, "American friends."

When we left Le Truel we rode along the Tarn River to the Dourdou River and turned east along the bank of the river to Saint Affrique. When we arrived in Saint Affrique the streets in town were blocked by a very unusual sight, a large truck with a second trailer was stuck. When the driver attempted to make a turn, somehow he had managed to get the signal light, which was on a post in the intersection, caught between the two trailers. Thus he could not move the truck or release the trailers. We managed to get through this town on the side-walks and through a crowd of people watching the event unfold.

From here we came up short of Le Caylor in the quiet town of Carnus at the headwaters of the Serguis River. We were at a street corner where the street was filled with cars, busses, children, bicycles, walkers, flies and insects of all the kinds.

We decided on a long ride the next day leaving Carnus early and heading for Gegnac about 90 kms.. We had read about the "Devils Footprint" in France, a deep canyon much like our Grand Canyon. Cirque de Navacelles, is a circular hole in the earth with a river running through the canyon. The road down to the bottom is a circle road that clings to the sides of the canyon. We decided we could observe the canyon from the top while we enjoyed lunch. After lunch I did some creative map reading to avoid retracing our steps, and took road D

130 from Cirque de Navacelles. While stopping to make sure we were on the correct road, I noticed a "Dolmen formation" on the map. I told Ann to keep an eye out for the formation, she looked to her right and pointed to the Dolmen formation, almost untouched by tourists. So different than Ireland, where the tourists had built smaller dolmens all around the main structure. After that excitement we continued down D 130 into the town of Navacelles and came to a dead end. It took a while to find the road to leave town. About 5 kms. out of town we spotted two large boulders, one on either side of the road. When we rode between the boulders, the bottom dropped out and opened up to an amazing view. We could see forever! How easily we had climbed so high. But there we stood overlooking a vast valley. From there we did not turn a crank for 30 kms. into the town of Gignac. This is a region for float trips on the Herauit River. Since it was summer, the town was complete, full. We rode to a campground and asked for a place to camp, the owner said, "Complete!" I said "très petit," very small. The owner smiled and motioned for us to come with him. He found a place we could set up our tent and we motioned OK! Just as he was leaving he said, "Tonight is Paella Night, would you like to eat with the camp?" "Yes!" When we showed up for dinner our names were written on the table, Ann on one side and me on the other, and best of all we were seated between four couples who spoke English. When the server came by we ordered water, no way, the four couples ordered wine for themselves and for us, and after a couple bottles of wine and a great dinner of paella, we attempted to excuse ourselves and leave the fun as we had to ride the next day.

When we stood and I asked for the check, the owner's wife came over and said "The price is, you have to sing for your supper." I looked at Ann and we began to attempt to think of a song to sing, finally the owners wife said, "Sing your National Anthem." "No, let's think of something else," we could not, so we began to sing the National Anthem, everyone stood, we got stuck on the words and stopped, everyone sat down, we started again, everyone stood up, we got stuck on the words again and everyone sat down. The next morning it was as if everyone knew us as old friends and gave us a roaring send off.

We had read about Aigues-Mortes, a walled city. It appeared much as it was when built in the 1200's except now it turned out to be a tourist trap. After a short visit we were off to Saintes-Maries-de-la-Mer. This was the flattest part of France we had bicycled through to date. There was one problem with Saintes-Maries-de-la-Mer, it was like Coney Island. There were plenty of things to do and we did them. Took a ride along the coast, a boat ride up the Le Petit Rhône, where we saw as promised the white horses and black bulls of the Camargue as well as the pink flamingos. As the boat cruised up the Le Petit Rhône, it slowed and the crew began to toss baguettes on to the shore. Out of the woods came the white horses and black bulls of the Camargue. Ann and I laughed at the hokie cruise we had taken.

Now the bull fight was something else. It was held in a Roman arena from the time when the Romans ruled this part of the world. The first event involved the ladies of the Camargue. They were dressed in gowns with beautiful handmade mantillas, worn over a high comb called a peineta. They stood in a circle around the arena holding a tray with an orange placed in the middle of the tray. The cowboys were timed as they broke from the starting gate and rode around the arena picking off the oranges from each tray and tossing them into the audience. It just so happened that the first cowboy tossed the first orange straight at Ann. We sat watching this orange come toward her face, suddenly a hand from the man in front of us caught the orange. Before each cowboy broke from the starting gate the announcer would call out, "juice de orange." Ann said, "It wasn't real was it?" "Oh!" "Yes you were almost juice de orange." When the real part of the bullfight started, it continued to get more and more exciting as the older bullfighters and the better bulls were released. Then with one leap, the bull was over the first wall around the arena. As the bull ran around the arena the bullfighters inside the wall leapt over into the arena. This brought cheers from the crowd and ended the show. In France they do not kill or harm the bulls, the fighters appear to come out on the losing end of the fight.

When we started our ride across France people would ask, "Where are you riding to?" "We will end our ride in Marseilles." "Oh!" "Do not go to Marseilles, it is a bad place." This we were told all the way across France. Our final stop would be in a town short of Marseilles by the name of Chateauneuf les Martigues. We would be staying in a B&B run by Madame Tyna Levrault and Jacque, her gentleman friend, who did the cooking. They entertained us for the last week we were in France.

We rented a car and began to enjoy the Mediterranean coast, the beaches, and the wonderful food. The first time we headed out to a beach, Madame Tyna Levrault directed us to a family beach, where the women were still topless but the men had swim-trunks on, not like one of the nude beaches. She also sent us to a restaurant for Bouillabaisse. Julia Child, who lived in Marseille for a year, wrote: "to me the telling flavor of bouillabaisse comes from two things: the Provençal soup base—garlic, onions, tomatoes, olive oil, fennel, saffron, thyme, bay, and usually a bit of dried orange peel—and, of course, the fish—lean (non-oily), firm-fleshed, soft-fleshed, gelatinous, and shellfish." Because of all the ingredients in the bouillabaisse, our reservations were made several days in advance and we had to cover the charge before they would honor the reservations. It was worth the experience. We ate on the top of a restaurant, accompanied by many cats, yes cats. Ann is a cat lover and enjoyed the sights and sounds of the cats, they were not friendly but they were around.

We also cruised along the coast and then we did the unthinkable, we drove into Marseilles. Now we had been told over and over that it was a bad place. Mistakenly, we did not lock the car doors as we drove through Marseilles. As we were stopped at a red light a scooter came up behind us. He had been following us for quite a few blocks and for whatever reason, and our good luck, I closed the gap between our car and the parked cars along the street so he could not pass on the right side of the car, nor could he open the door wide enough to get into the car easily. There were two riders on the scooter, the taller and larger rider suddenly appeared at the door on Ann's side of the car, and pulled the door open. Ann had all the maps on top of her purse on the floor of the car. He knew where women place their purses and began to search for the purse. When he found the purse, Ann and I had one end of the strap and he had the other. I also grabbed the back of his helmet, it just happened to be one with a solid strap under the chin, and around his head. As I pulled on the strap on the purse it began to tear but I had his head and began to pull even harder, he pulled his head free. I had his helmet but he had Ann's purse. I jumped from the car, the scooter began to run off without the thief or the purse. I was gaining on the scooter when I heard a voice of authority call "Halt masseur, halt" when I turned to look, the purse was in the street, the helmet was in the street, and beautiful blue police uniforms were also lying in the street. They were two off duty policemen who came to our rescue. I picked up the uniforms, the finest of silk and yet they had dropped them to help catch the thief. We got the purse back.

When Ann and I were at an ATM trying to draw enough money for the last few days in France, we made the mistake of withdrawing not 500 francs but 5,000 francs, instead of having $100.00, in the purse we had $1,000.00 in the purse, and that was one reason we were fighting so hard to hold on to the purse. The police gave Ann her purse, saving her passport and other papers.

The police also took us back to the police headquarters to make a report. We found later that the two police who saved us in Marseilles received a commendation for their work. So it turned out Marseilles was a bad place but not at the B&B. We received a hero's welcome when we returned and the owners discovered our mishap. That night we had a BBQ French style, grilled steaks.

The next day we had to pack to come home and needed boxes for our panniers. The boxes for the bicycles were furnished by Delta airline. We arrived in Dublin in May and now we were leaving Marseilles in July ahead of the school holidays in France. Never attempt to vacation in France in August. So, we began to look for boxes, and spotted a building with the words MOVING across the front. That should be just the place, no the MOVING store was an exercise gym and the MOVING was for the people at the gym to MOVE. We shared many laughs at ourselves in France. We did discover the correct place, picked up the boxes and packed for home.

When we arrived at the Marseilles Airport, Delta Airlines gave us boxes for the bicycles. Now we were all packed to leave France, one other thing, we had to move all the boxes, and bicycles to the gate, and we did. Then I had to go back to the ticket desk one more time to get everything straight. We were going to fly Air France to Paris and then

Delta to the USA. As I was making the changes, a lady, ok, not so much a lady, ran up to me and said, "Monsieur, do you speak English?" "Oui, a little bit." "Thank God I have found a God Damn Frenchman who can speak English." "Just what do we have to do to get out of here?" "Do you see that man standing over there?" "Yes so what?" "If you will take your luggage and your ticket over to him, he will put you on that plane for Paris and you will get out of here." "A little bit! A little bit!" As she crossed the airport for the Air France boarding ramp I noticed her companion, a very meek man walking behind her as she explained how they were going to get out of Marseilles.

We also boarded the plane for Paris and were instructed to retrieve our luggage in Paris to recheck the luggage for the USA. Moving luggage from one side of an airport as large as the Paris Charles de Gaulle Airport was not an easy job, and rechecking at the Delta ticket desk was not an easy job, or arriving in Atlanta, GA and reclaiming our luggage to go through Customs, was not an easy job. So getting home from Europe in 2001 was an adventure in itself. Whew! It was really nice to be back home!

2002 Ride Across the USA #2
Florence, Oregon to York Town, Virginia

On September 11, 2001 everyone's lives changed in some way. In our home the world had always been our oyster and all we had to do was enjoy it. Suddenly we were afraid to travel abroad. We worried about air travel. We sat home wondering what to do. Should we take a chance and travel among the people who had decided to terrorize us or just stay home and feel safe. Ann and I love to ride our bicycles long distances. In 1999 we rode from Seattle Washington to Bar Harbor Maine. We began to remember how much fun we had had riding across the USA. Why not do it again and to heck with Europe. Why put ourselves in harm's way? So we rented a car, loaded all our toys and set out on two great adventures.

First we would hike rim to rim across the Grand Canyon. We would ship all our hiking gear home and continue to Florence, Oregon.

Second we would dip the back tires of our bicycles into the Pacific Ocean and head to York Town, Virginia to dip the front tires in the Atlantic Ocean. This ride would take us three months and six days and we would ride 4,433 miles across ten states. You are probably thinking what do we get out of riding a bicycle across the country? We have learned the kindness of people and the desire to help people in need stretches from coast to coast.

a. Mom's pie shop

Every bicyclists we met from Florence to Mom's Pie Shop told us about the best pies between the two oceans. The destination was the McKenzie River Valley and Mom's Pie Shop. It seemed that all the bicyclists from the east coast heading west had on their minds was pie and also they were keeping a log of the best pie and pie shops and Mom's Pie Shop was the best. They should know for they had ridden about 4,000 miles to reach Mom's Pie Shop and they had passed a lot of pie shops. As we rode along the McKenzie River, we heard the sounds of turkeys up on the hillside and I explained how my grandfather and an uncle had taught me how to call a turkey. This was nothing new to Ann, who already knew how to call a turkey in the wild from her experience in Montana.

Now it was my turn and I began to call as I had been taught and sure enough the turkeys began to come down the hillside, I was really feeling my oats. Just as they were about twenty feet above our heads, a car came along the highway and they spooked and flew across the McKenzie River. If you have never heard a turkey fly, ride a bike and spook a turkey. They really make a lot of noise when they fly.

Now back to the pie, for the pie shop was just up the road and a nice riverside cabin also was close by the pie shop. We checked into the cabin and walked to Mom's Pie Shop, where we had dinner and the Red, White, and Blue pie. It was a raspberry and blueberry with a white filling and sure enough the bicyclists we had met along the way told us the truth. It was the best pie and the best pie shop between Florence, OR and York Town, VA.

b. Henry's pussy

In Mitchell, Oregon, we were welcomed at a local B&B by a large black cat. It stayed around as long as the owners of the B&B were not present. When the owners arrived the cat disappeared. The owners apologized for not being present when we arrived but explained they had to go into a nearby town to see a doctor. The B&B was open when we arrived and a note explained this to us. That was the reason we waited for their return. When the apologies were over we said, "That is OK, we had a beautiful cat to pet, is it your cat?" "No, that's Henry's pussy." "Who is Henry?" "You'll have to ask at the bar next door." That we did and to our surprise the response was, "Henry, is the local bear, and the cat sleeps with Henry, so it is his pussy." "What bear?" We found out they had a very large black bear in a cage, because someone had de-clawed the bear. The town had built a large cage for Henry, the bear and he had his own pussy.

Some of the kindness began shortly after beginning our ride. In Mitchell, Oregon, we met a group of people having a gospel music event. We could attend for the price of a pie. They greeted us as one of their own and we enjoyed the music and the pies. I love sweets.

Further along the ride we arrived in Dayville, Oregon. There was nowhere to stay, not even a city park to camp in. We had talked to other bicyclists along the way and learned that in Dayville, the women of Dayville had made bicyclists their mission. They had turned the Dayville Presbyterian Church into an overnight stay for bicyclists. Showers, kitchen, laundry room, and we could sleep anywhere we wanted to in the church except on the pews or remove the pew pads. That was our first time to sleep in a church. We have slept in our own church many times since, as Germantown Presbyterian Church is host for the homeless sponsored by Memphis Interfaith Association. Ann and I give our time because someone cared enough to open their church and their hearts so we would have a dry and warm place to sleep.

When we reached the top of Lolo Pass we were met by a large motorcycle club out for a joy ride. As I reached the top of the pass one of the bikers looked around and said, "You're the first bicyclist I've ever seen with a smile on his face after climbing any pass." I said "Just wait and you will see the second bicyclist with a smile for climbing this pass." Sure enough when Ann rode up she had an even bigger smile than I had had and the bikers began to laugh and we joined in. We looked back down the pass and realized we had just ridden 100 miles up a mountain pass where Lewis and Clark had traveled two hundred years ago but we did it on bicycles.

The laughter we shared with each other turned into praise and thanks to God for giving us our health and the strength to accomplish the ride over Lolo Pass.

c. My hair cut in Baker City

This route takes bicyclists through Baker City, Oregon. As we approached Baker City, Ann suggested I get a haircut. So, that afternoon upon our arrival, I went out in search of a place to get a haircut. Soon I saw a hair salon and walked inside, where there was one young man "styling" a man's hair and I inquired if he took walk-ins, "Yes." So, I asked if I could be next in line. I was, so, I sat, read, and prepared myself for the hair cut to come. No, I did not prepare myself for the hair cut to come, no-one on earth could have prepared themselves for the hair cut I received. After being seated in the "salon chair" the young man asked how I liked my hair cut. "Well, my barber back home---" "I beg your pardon." "I am not a barber." "I am a stylist." "Well," I began again attempting to explain how I liked my hair cut and after using the "B" word too many times, the "stylist" hit me upside the head with the clippers and skinned my head up to a nice circle around the top and announced he had completed the job. I attempted to protest and to threaten him with not paying and he returned with "You will either pay or deal with the Baker City's finest." I paid. I also had a desert hat, the kind with the flap that protects one's neck from the sun, and one's hair from being seen.

d. Leaving Cody

This hair cut would not grow out until Kentucky. Along the way we would pass through Wyoming and the home town of

State Representative Buck Aurty, who proposed and passed the law to prohibit RV's for one week on the state highways in Wyoming. Meeteetse, Wyoming is about thirty-five miles south of Cody. Ann and I had already ridden across Wyoming in 1995, through Jackson Hole and along the Snake River. We decided not to repeat that part of the Centennial Route but to do some creative map reading and head to Cody, south to Meeteetse, on to Thermopiles, south over Beaver Ridge Pass (9% grade for 3 miles after a 29 mile climb to the Ridge and no payback) and reconnect to the Centennial Route in Jeffrey City, Wyoming. Well, Meeteetse is not half way to Thermopolis and Thermopolis is too far for us to ride in one day. We decided to stay over in Meeteetse. This was a lazy day, slow riding, for a short thirty-mile day. As we departed Cody, we came upon a crossing arm raised on the side of the highway with a sign stating if the arm was down, a fine of $150.00 would be placed on anyone going around the arm. We wondered, was it for flooding, wind or just snow? No more thought was given to the crossing arm as we rode into Meeteetse and spotted the Broken Spoke Cafe, a great lunch spot, dinner too, but breakfast had to be somewhere else, because they were not open for breakfast. When my helmet came off, on came the desert cap, my mother taught me to remove my hat when eating but she had never seen me with a haircut the likes of which I had received in Baker City.

e. Mateesee, WY and my hat

I wore my cap during lunch. After lunch as we walked out the front door of the Broken Spoke, across the street sat a cowboy, boots, hat, spurs, and wrinkles, just as anyone would expect in a cowboy. He cocked his head to one side and said, "Can I ask you a question?" "Sure." "Just what in the hell do you have on your head?" "Well, I have a desert cap and it is not coming off." "Oh!" "I'm sorry, I shouldn't have asked, I'm always putting my two cents in where it doesn't belong." "That's OK, no harm." As I stated earlier, the Broken Spoke was closed for breakfast so we went to Lucille's Cafe for breakfast, and as we walked inside I spotted the cowboy sitting at the "good-ole boys table." Every small town cafe has such a table and Ann and I have learned not to take that table even when there was no one at the table, but this morning the local men's group had gathered, the table was full and there sat the cowboy from the day before. I only had my helmet on and no desert cap to cover the sins of the Baker City haircut. I walked over to the local table and said, "Hello," to the cowboy and began to explain how my mother would want me to eat breakfast without a helmet on and when I removed my helmet, I did not want to spot anyone laughing about my hair cut. Cowboy, began to apologize for the day before, I explained that I understood and turned to walk to a booth. The local leader of the "good-ole boy table" spoke up with, "I see you have already met George." "Yes," "I met him yesterday when I had my desert cap on and attempted to explain my hair cut." "I will let all of you know I take offence at anyone laughing at my hair cut and I am about to remove my helmet." I removed my helmet to the roar of laughter and the question, "Did you really pay for that hair cut?" "Yes." The leader began to explain that George had gone to Cody and come home with much the same type haircut and then he explained who George was. You see Biff on the David Letterman show had thrown a dart at the United States and hit Meeteetse, Wyoming and Biff and camera crew had come to Meeteetse to see what goes on in Meeteetse, and George was the recipient of the interview from Biff. By the time Biff had finished with George, they had to bleep everything George had said. That was my cowboy who welcomed us into Meeteetse, but enough is not enough, as Ann decided to ask about the crossing arm just outside of Cody. She asked the leader of the table, "When we departed Cody, there was a crossing arm that stated, if the arm is down, a fine of $150.00 would be placed on anyone going around the arm. We were wondering, is it for flooding, wind or just snow?" "Oh!" "My word that is how you got here, the arm was up, it is supposed to keep that bunch of riff raff bicyclists out of Meeteetse." We all laughed and if you ever get a chance to visit Meeteetse, ask for George.

On the cover of the menu for Lucille's Cafe is a "Black-footed ferret." When the server came, I asked, "Do you have Black-footed ferrets around here?" The good ole boy's table answered, "Not anymore!" The leader spoke up again and explained. There was a rancher near Meeteetse who shot a Black-footed ferret and brought it into a local taxidermist to have it mounted, because he thought it was so beautiful. Then the taxidermist explained to the rancher that he had killed an endangered animal and he had to report the killing to the government. This he did, but the rancher said, "They ain't in danger, my ranch is alive with these things." The government knew Black-footed ferrets did not belong in Meeteetse, they belonged in Colorado. The government then sent a team of trappers to Meeteetse, they trapped the Black-footed ferrets and moved them back to Colorado where they belonged. Thus, the statement, "Not anymore!"

Wyoming is one of the states we would love to return to ride, the wide-open spaces, the beauty of the state, and yes, most of all the wonderful people me met along the ride. Now we want to return in July and ride without any RV's to pass us or frighten us off the road. Stop and think who is driving those big rigs. I am in my eighties, retired and sat at a desk most of my life. I would hate to think I had to learn to drive an over-sized vehicle at eighty. Most of the drivers of the large RV's are retired and most sat behind a desk, and now they are the one's driving those over-sized rigs. There are no laws regarding training for driving such rigs and no age limits for drivers. Just think what it would be like to ride without large RV's on the highways. Go to Wyoming in July and enjoy the greatest week on American highways. During the week of July 16 to July 22, except on Interstates 80, 25, and 90, over-sized campers such as motor homes, fifth wheels and vacation camper trailers are not allowed on state highways. It started out as a joke by State Representative Buck Aurty. He even voted against the law and attempted to persuade Governor Fred N. Thal to veto the law. He did not and now there is a week without RV's in Wyoming. The Governor stated, "If they want to come to Wyoming during that week they can get a horse'ie."

f. Meeteese to Saratoga

From Meeteese we rode to Thermopolis, and enjoyed the thermal pool as we knew the next day would be a challenge. From Thermopolis, south over Beaver Ridge Pass and then we would reconnect to the Centennial Route in Jeffrey City, Wyoming. Jeffrey City was a booming mining town just a few years before we arrived but not anymore. The buildings were sold, dismantled and moved away leaving only the foundations as reminder that a town once stood there. The only thing left was a "Bar Room Saloon" just like the old west, oh! And one other thing, a motel, crude but a motel. When we arrived we stopped at the "Bar Room Saloon" and the owner informed us we needed to beat the Mormons to the motel as they would be "podding up" when they arrived later in the afternoon. They did! Of course, we had the bar to ourselves and a good dinner but were mostly alone.

When we returned to the motel, I thought it would be simple enough to lock the bicycles to a tree in front of our door, no way. The owner, a lady about our age came out in a huff and informed me to keep the bicycles off of her tree, so I took the bicycles into our room for the night.

The next day we had to ride the Interstate Highway as that is the only highway heading from Jeffrey City toward Saratoga, Wyoming. In Saratoga we were greeted to free internet service by the Chamber of Commerce of Saratoga. They were also having Toga Days and a five-kilometer race. We joined in the race and Ann and I won our age group. We were given a beautiful leather tooled award for our efforts. The airport in Saratoga can accommodate any size airplane and had a landing strip larger than most cities. We found out the Senator form Wyoming lived in Saratoga. He and his friends love to fish and this was one of the best fishing spots in Wyoming. So his friends can fly into Saratoga in any size airplane.

g. Entering Colorado

We had expected wide shoulders on the highways in Colorado like those in Wyoming, but NO SHOULDERS! Surprise! We entered Colorado on a narrow two-lane highway without a bicycle lane, or shoulder to ride on along the highway. We had heard so much about the good bicycling in Colorado I suppose we expected too much from the entire state. Now, there are better places to bicycle in Colorado but not to travel by bicycle across the state. Also along the way we encountered road construction, really down to the bare earth and not like Montana where they gave us a ride through the construction zone. In Colorado they left the passage up to us. Somewhere along the way before we reached Breckenridge, I split a wheel, not a flat, a wheel. When I was attempting to air up my tire I noticed the tube coming out the side of the wheel and stopped pumping the tire, let the air out and discovered the long split in the wheel. No problem, we were in bicycle country! Wrong, wrong kind of bicycling, mountain bicycling, not touring bicycles. As I talked to the owner of the bicycle shop about a wheel, one of the employees remembered they had ordered a wheel for a customer and he had never picked it up and that it had been in stock for several years. Great, saved, they took my hub and rebuilt the wheel. We took a day off in Breckenridge, and to our surprise my brothers son, Robert Phillips, my nephew and his family came to cheer us along on our ride. They live in Cheyenne, WY. We were surprised that they would drive over to meet us but they did and we enjoyed a wonderful visit.

h. Over Hoosier Pass!

With a new wheel and a rest, we restarted our ride across the USA. Just ten miles out of Breckenridge, we had the highest mountain pass to cross, Hoosier Pass at 11,542 feet. Once over the pass we entered the town of Fairplay and met friends. Ann attended Mount Holyoke College, and a former classmate of hers had moved to Fairplay, CO, Barbara Lewis and her husband John, met us in Fairplay. We were able to store our bicycles and gear at the hotel in Fairplay and travel by car to their home in a remote part of the state of Colorado. Really remote, only one or two homes in the area as it was billed as a retirement community. They gave us a bed, shower, and a wonderful dinner. The next day we took a seven-mile hike, and a drive to a couple of ghost towns. They had a state of the art home with a view of the Collegiate Range of the Rocky Mountains. Their home faced Mt. Princeton.

Two days later we arrived in Cañon City and stopped at the Parkview Motel. Dinner that evening was Italian at Di Rito's restaurant. After dinner we decided to see the only movie in town, "Signs" starring Mel Gibson. Now remember this movie for later on it will appear in this book for a good laugh.

The next day we stopped at the Royal Gorge, walked the bridge and rode 56 miles to Pueblo. Do you remember back in 1999 when we passed through Columbia Falls, MT, we were rescued by Lonnie and George Parsons? Surprise! They now live in Raton Pass, NM, and they were meeting us in Pueblo. We have met so many wonderful people as we bicycle around the world and hope to keep making friends for many more years hopefully by bicycle. We had dinner and breakfast together and we were off, well not really. I had a flat coming into Pueblo on my front wheel and now I had a flat on the back wheel as we were leaving, so a little delay. With the delay, we rode only 55 miles into Ordway, CO. Both of us had "gas" I'm talking serious gas, so off to the drug store for help. While we were there the pharmacist began to tell us where to eat dinner, "fried spaghetti" at the Saucer Block, the restaurant had been in town since the 1800's. With our problem, fried anything did not sound good but we tried the fried spaghetti and it caused more gas, well that is enough about that problem. Two days later we arrived in Tribune, KS. We had completed 2,283 miles with another 2,000+ miles to go but we are in Kansas, Dorothy!

i. Bazine to the rescue

Our greatest blessing came in Kansas. We had planned to ride forty-six miles the next day but we arrived in Scott City before 11 A.M. and decided to make up a day by riding another fifty-seven miles to Ness City. When we arrived, the town was full of antique cars and all the hotels were full, no room in the inn. The camp ground was the pits and we felt we could not stay there. We went to a local restaurant and asked one of the waitresses if she knew of a place in town or anyone who would put up a couple bicyclists for the night. She called her pastor but no answer, then a lady in the restaurant spoke up and said "You two look so honest, if you don't mind riding another sixteen miles I have a house in Bazine you can sleep in for the night. My husband's sister has passed away and the house is just as she left it and you can sleep on the back porch if you wish." We wished, then she said "Now you'll have to eat here as there's nowhere to eat in Bazine. How long do you think it will take you to arrive in Bazine." I guessed a couple hours with eating and when we arrived, Marian was waiting for us with food for breakfast. Then we had a long conversation to find out just who she had asked to sleep in her husband's sister's house. We passed the test and I asked her if we could pay her, all she said was "Send me a Christmas card." I took her name and address. Oh! By the way if you were keeping track of how many miles we rode that day it was 119 miles on loaded bicycles. Our best one day ride ever, of course we were in Kansas and it is flat but we also had a strong wind at our backs.

Now back to the Christmas card. I could not find her address. I stewed over what to do as I was determined that Marian would receive her card. I decided to call the sheriff's office in Bazine and ask if they knew a lady named Marian, no last name, lived on a cattle ranch and attended the local Methodist Church. The sheriff said "Oh that must be Marian Kleweno." I asked for her address and phone number. I called, Marian answered the phone, when I said "Hello" she said "Roscoe I would know your strong southern voice anywhere." I said "You have just saved me a drive to Bazine, for I was going to get you a Christmas card even if I had to drive to Bazine and hand deliver it to you." She said "You don't want to come to Bazine, we are in the middle of a blizzard. It is snowing so hard we cannot see the barn from the house, stay in Tennessee and mail me that card." This was in 2002, almost twenty years ago and we have exchanged Christmas cards until 2019. I mailed my card to her but did not receive a card from her. Her husband had Parkinson's and was in a nursing home in Ness City. I did not know how Marian was or why she had not sent me a card or why my card had not been returned. Then a surprise, in March 2021, as I was writing this part of the book, I received a letter from Marian. Marian's husband had passed away and she has the cattle ranch with her sons. I am so sorry for her loss, but we are still in touch. I will send her a copy of this book.

j. Miles to go Across Kansas

After a day of 119 miles, we were still eager to cross Kansas and began several long mileage days, first from Bazine to Larned a distance of 64 miles, then Larned to Hutchinson, 75 more miles and a day off in Hutchinson. Remember we had stopped in Cañon City, Colorado and watched Mel Gibson in the movie "Signs." It was filmed in a corn field where the aliens cut signs in the corn field, this is the part where it fits into our story. Somewhere between Larned and Hutchinson Ann had to go, you know, get relief. Ann asked "What should I do?" I said "Just go down in the corn field, no one is around."

She walked into the corn field, and right back out, I asked, "What happened, you did not have enough time to do your thing?" "It sounds just like the sound in that movie we saw in Cañon City." "You mean "Signs?" "Yes and I cannot go in there." Finally we did reach a gas station and the Aliens did not capture her in Kansas.

Now back to Hutchinson, as we approached a storm was about to hit the town. Black is black when in Kansas and a storm was brewing. Lightening is brighter and straighter in Kansas and it always looked like Dorothy was coming to The Land of Oz. We grabbed the first motel, a Super 8 Motel and we were out of the storm, we thought, but just as we got into our room, the managers began to hustle everyone into the basement. The storm knocked out the electrical power in that part of Hutchinson. We could not return to our rooms as the room keys would not work. We did have emergency lighting in the basement and were able to escape to the first floor.

The next day we found a bicycle shop, purchased new tires for Ann's bicycle and had the brakes adjusted. We also visited the Space Center. From Hutchinson to Newton, only 35 miles, but it was Ann's birthday and we wanted to celebrate. The next day a ride of 74 miles and dinner that evening at the Paddock Restaurant. It was named for the thoroughbred racing from May to July in Eureka. The next day was another long day, 65 miles to Chanute. Somewhere in between Eureka and Chanute was the town of Buffalo, and with some creative map reading I found a country road that led to a state fishing lake and park, a great place to eat lunch. During that stop, along came Mr. Yarnell. Mr. Yarnell had lived in this part of Kansas since 1922. He arrived there newly married and in a place with no indoor plumbing, no running water, and no electricity. We had lots to talk about as I was raised in much the same conditions. Mr. Yarnell was driving a pair of beautiful horses, Haflingers, light tan and beautiful does not begin to describe them. After a very long talk, we really had to ride as we were still short of our destination.

k. Kansas in a barn

From Chanute, we headed to Golden City, MO. But our day did not turn out to be as we planned. The sky looked as if Dorothy was about to travel to The Land of Oz and we needed a place to hide. I noticed a farmer on his tractor coming to the storage shed, and asked if we could hide from the storm. He said, "Get in the milk barn, it is clean." So we hid for the day in his milk barn. The barn was about three miles short of Erie. After the storm, we rode into Erie and checked into The Land of Oz Motel, well not really. They did not have to pay for the name as they spelled it "The Land of Ahs Motel." We had ridden only 19 miles, as we spent most of the day in the farmer's barn just short of Erie, KS, known as "Beantown USA." They have a large bean festival each year and bean cook-off. This would be our last night in Kansas. It was 79 miles from Erie, Kansas to Golden City, MO. Golden City knew how to treat bicyclists! They had a bicyclists hostel, with a shower, TV, movies, cooking area, bicycle storage and repair shop. We felt pampered.

l. Missouri and the Red-necks come out

If you think all of America loves bicyclists, just ride across Missouri. From the time we entered the state we were told to "Get the F__k off the road," almost all day long, every day. We were so tired of getting the "finger" and cussed for riding a bicycle we wanted to stop our ride but Ann and I were not quitters. I will even fast forward to Chester, IL. We crossed into Illinois and on our first day of riding in Illinois, a car came by with all four windows down and four arms out of the windows with the "finger" standing tall, I said, "Oh no not in Illinois too," but the car had Missouri plates. The cussing and fingers stopped after that and we finished our ride to York Town, VA without hearing the F word again.

m. Not all is Bad in Missouri

I have already told you about the wonderful bicycle hostel in Golden City, MO. Well there were a lot of other things that made it possible to ride in Missouri without screaming bloody murder. In Ash Grove, MO we checked into the Maple Tree B&B. We were now in the northern part of the Ozark Mountains and it was hill after hill, straight down and straight back up, there were no switch backs. Ann said, "This is like riding in and out of Big Hill Pond State Park all day." Now you will have to go to Big Hill Pond State Park, TN and discover the reason for the statement.

On August 20, we rode 39 miles, arrived in Marshfield early and celebrated our thirteenth anniversary. Another 70 miles the next day took us to Houston, MO and closer to getting out of Missouri. From Houston, to Eminence and on to Centerville, and to a campground from HELL. Yes, a real outhouse, water pump, and plenty of trash, as the campground had not been cleaned for years much less used. So we did what we have done in the past when we needed a better place to stay. Centerville does not have a hotel, motel, or B&B. We went to the library and asked the lady at the library if she knew anyone who had a place where we could stay, and that is how Clovis Motts, entered our lives.

n. Clovis and the Underground House

A lady searching for a book to read, heard our conversation and spoke up, "I live six miles out of town and I have a room and would enjoy your company this evening. I would like to hear about your bicycle ride across the USA." I let her know we would be pleased to pay her for her trouble, "No way." "You will have to follow me and I will wait at each turn for you to appear and that will get you to my house. It is a little hard to find as it is under ground." We learned that Clovis Motts' husband had been an architect and had designed this house to be built underground so it did not need any heat or air conditioning. The walls were all concrete, so there was little chance of a fire. That evening Clovis cooked trout for our dinner, and served us a great breakfast of blueberry pancakes. She would not accept anything when I offered to pay. Remember this was 2002, about a year after 9-11 and kindness lived along the route we rode across the USA that year, and for years to follow as we continued to meet kindness almost everywhere we bicycled.

Clovis also wanted a Christmas card, I did not lose her address and we stayed in touch until 2014 when we received our Christmas card returned with no forwarding address. She was a lovely lady and I miss her cards.

o. Crossing the Mississippi River at Chester, IL

The first trip across the USA we waded across the Mississippi River at Lake Itasca Minnesota, now we were faced with a bridge, floored with see-through steel mesh, and all this on 26 mm tires. We made it with Ann worrying all the way across the bridge as we could see the River below. This was a lot different from wading across the same River about 700 miles north of Chester, IL.

Chester, is the Spinach Capital and home of "Popeye the Sailor Man." He was standing at the end of the bridge when we rode into Chester. He welcomes everyone into town. We were out of Missouri and into a much friendlier atmosphere on the roads of Illinois. We had ridden 3,169 miles from Florence, OR.

We would make only two stop-overs in Illinois, first in Carbondale and then in Elizabethtown. As we were entering Elizabethtown, a couple young boys came riding up beside me and I said, "Want to race?" "Yeah!" We were off me on a loaded bicycle but with better gears, and wheels. The race was down the middle of Main Street, and the people on the sides of the street were cheering the boys on to victory. Yes, they won. Or at least one of the boys, the others faltered long before we got to the end of the race. The roar for the local boy went up. By the time we finished the race I was standing in the street facing the River Rose Inn with the B&B behind me. Don Phillips, no kin, had been watching the race, also he was the owner of the River Rose Inn, but we had already made reservations to stay in the B&B, it was a welcome sight. That evening we ate dinner on a river barge in the Ohio River.

p. Taking the Ferry to Kentucky

Just two states left to cross to reach the Atlantic Ocean, Kentucky and Virginia and we will have completed crossing the USA twice. Our first stop on the way to Kentucky was the Cave in the Rock State Park and then on to the ferry for a ride across the Ohio River. Our day was short, just 24 miles to Marion, KY. We stopped at a B&B and sat on the porch reading and writing in our journals until we figured out that they were closed. Then we went to a local motel, run by an Indian couple from Punjabi. On Thursday we rode 65 miles to Diamond Lake Resort in West Louisville. Now getting to the resort was a hoot as we asked in Sebree, if they knew any place to stay, no, then on to Beach Grove and that was where we were directed to the Diamond Lake Resort, which had a great "watering hole."

We had two wonderful friends in Murfreesboro, Tennessee, Sid and Dot Cromwell, had because Sid has passed away but in 2002, Sid and Dot were very much alive and active. They were our bicycling buddies in Tennessee and now they were waiting for us in Rough River State Park, Kentucky. Since they travel in a motor home, we shared their motor home and enjoyed a couple days in the Park. After a great breakfast, and a long good-bye, Ann and I headed to Rolling Fork, to visit Abe Lincoln's birth place. 45 miles later we were in Old Bardstown Motel in Bardstown, the home of "My Ole Kentucky Home" where Stephen Foster wrote the song.

The ride was easier than any since we entered Missouri and faced the rolling hills of the Ozarks. 57 miles later we were checking into a Shaker Village in Pleasant Hill, this was Kentucky horse country. The Shaker Village is five miles off route along Mays Creek. This is where the Adventure Cycle route should run. Shaker Village of Pleasant Hill was established in 1821. This is a wonderful vacation place for anyone especially a family, as the music show was great, the lectures on how the Shakers lived and a boat ride on the Kentucky River made this a wonderful place to stop for the night or a vacation.

Our next stopover was in Berea, Kentucky. We had been looking forward to our return to Berea from the time we planned this ride. One of the things we did for Thanksgiving was to take a trip, and in 1991, we stopped at the Boon Tavern

Inn in Berea for Thanksgiving Day. We were in our warm-ups and asked about dinner, "NOT DRESSED LIKE THAT." "Then how should we dress?" "Coat and tie for you, and DRESS for the lady" "We have them in the car," "You may change in the rest rooms and I will hold a table for you." We did and we had the best roast lamb we have ever had for Thanksgiving. We bought a "Skiddles game" from Berea College, and still enjoy playing the game. Now we are back in Berea and checking into Boon Tavern for the night, we got a Master Suite for $59.00, a bargain.

Downhill always sounds good, and that is what we got from Berea to Boonville, and surprise, the Fair was going on in Boonville. We walked around the fair, ate dinner at Dooley's a place for steak, but do not order steak, order the Reese's Pie and forget everything else on the menu. The next day we encountered the Cushaw Festival in Chavies. You have no idea how many ways the cushaw can be cooked, carved, and enjoyed, but the people of Chavies did and the party went on. We could not find a place to stay in Chavies, so we moved on out of town to the Alice Lloyd College Hostel in Pippa Passes. Unfortunately the building the hostel was located in was rotting down and they did not seem to realize it. The floor sagged, the bunks on the wall were falling off but we were inside and we did have a shower.

Elkhorn City was our last stop in Kentucky. We are told not to stay with Mr. Moore as his motel was not up to par. Wrong, it was clean. The dinner and breakfast next door were southern style, all MUSH.

q. Over the Blue Ridge Parkway and Across Virginia

Our last day in Kentucky was a repeat of Missouri. It started out that way when a black, dented, noisy, t-top, Firebird decided to open the door an give us a fright. They pulled out of the right lane, close to Ann and then the door came open in an attempt to brush her off her bike. I yelled to alert her and she moved off the shoulder of the road. I was next and the door was wide open by the time they reached me, but I also managed to get off the road. After they had passed, we stopped and attempted to calm down, and wondered if it was really important enough to risk our lives riding in Virginia. We had made it through Missouri, but that was verbal with hand gestures, not wide open doors. That evening we checked into the Oak Motel. I began to look for a car rental but the phone book did not have a listing. So we did not end our ride in Rosedale, VA.

The next morning we met John and Betty from Branson Missouri, a couple bicycling the Centennial Bike Route, and again we received the best advice, "Keep going, you will regret it if you stop, do not let one ass-hole end your dream."

From Rosedale to Marion was the best of the best in bicycling. First a two-mile climb, then a seven mile pay-back downhill into Meadowview and lunch at the Oak's Diner. This whole day was a pleasure but the best came at the end of the ride when we rode through Hayters Gap. The road was along a creek at the bottom of the Gap with trees and vistas along the way. What a find, no harassment today.

Wednesday was another great day of bicycling and we ended the day in Newburn. The next day we arrived in Catawba and checked into the Down-Home B&B. Today's ride took us through another beautiful valley and we were pleased that we had continued our ride. We were directed to eat at "Home Place," a family style diner. All the bowls of food were placed on the table, a prayer was said, and then we could serve ourselves and pass food to each other, very southern.

A couple days later we arrived in Lexington, and promised each other a day off the bikes and a history lesson of the area. First to visit R. E. Lee's grave, then to VMI for more history. John and Betty had also taken a day off in Lexington. We had a good visit and lunch together along with a couple professors from Washington and Lee and more history lessons.

The next day we rode 53 miles, stopped in Afton, and moved on 28 miles to Charlottesville where we became celebrities. We stopped to visit Monticello, and were given the VIP treatment as they were celebrating the 200th anniversary of the Lewis and Clark Expedition. We were given T-shirts and free admission to Monticello.

Our next stop was 43 miles east in Louisa, and a stopover at the Whistle Stop B&B. The day before in Charlottesville we had paid double what it cost to stay at the Whistle Stop and here we had great hosts and a wonderful breakfast with a Baptist Minister. Then we rode out to face the day with a great ride to Ashland for lunch, and a night at the Henry Clay Inn. Friday morning we left Ashland for Charles City, rode along the James River and stayed at the Red Hill B&B. This would be our last full day of our trip across the USA. On 9/21/2002, after 4,433 miles we had arrived in Yorktown, VA. I had a flat! Oh! No! We could see the Atlantic Ocean and planned to dip our front tires in the Pacific Ocean. I pumped up the back tire enough to roll my bike out across the sand and dip the front tire alongside Ann. We were ready to return home after being away for four months and five days. Yes! It was Christmas, Thanksgiving, Birthdays and any other holiday rolled into one as we had accomplished something few couples have ever done, ridden from shore to shore across the USA for the second time.

2003 Helsinki
The Arctic Circle and Estonia

Like all great adventures, they begin with a dream. This one was no different. Ann read an article titled "Paradise of the North" about bicycling in Finland. This article was in the Adventure Cyclist, November/December 2002 issue. It was written by Sandy Duling and told about bicycle trails along each highway and through all the cities she rode through in Finland. It was about her ride in the southern part of Finland and taking the train to Rovaniemi, where she crossed the Arctic Circle. I thought what a great adventure it would be if we rode the perimeter of Finland from Helsinki to Rovaniemi and crossed the Arctic Circle as part of our ride, rather than taking the train to Rovaniemi. Then we would ride the last eight kilometers to the Arctic Circle. Ann agreed with me and we began to research the feasibility of making such a ride a reality. From Sandy's article we were able to get all the nuts and bolts of Finland's tourist information, bicycling maps, hostels, campgrounds and other guides about bicycling Finland.

Finland has a great system for bicycling, for every highway they build, they build a bike path alongside and separated from the highway. The paths have their own signal lights and stop signs for pedestrian cross-walks, other bike paths, and of course the highways. Most of the crossings are either under-passes or over-passes and the bicyclists do not come in contact with the traffic as they bike along. The only motorized vehicle using the paths is the Vespa or motor scooters. The paths are marked with route numbers, mile posts and directions. These bike routes have their own bridges across rivers and streams and we were never routed out on to the highway to use the traffic bridges. We have ridden in The Netherlands, which is 100% bike paths and bicyclists still have to deal with crossing traffic but not the case in Finland. In the northern part of Finland we did have to ride on unpaved roads with very little traffic but once a cyclist rides that far north it becomes a wonderful place to just enjoy the quiet of the forest and take advantage of the slower riding imposed by the unpaved roads. Life slows down in the northern part of Finland and it did for us as we rode through the northern forest.

Our dream of riding in Finland became a reality on May 29, 2003. We landed in Vantaa, Finland, home of the Helsinki airport, thirteen kilometers north of the city. We rode on bicycle paths from the airport to the Ramada International, Ramada Helsinki Airport, Vantaa, Finland. What a difference a bicycle path makes when riding out of an airport in any country. Think what it would take for a stranger, with no English, and maps written in English, to arrive at the Memphis International Airport and have to ride into the heart of Memphis. In Finland the paths are marked in Swedish, English and Finnish. Here in the United States, even as it becomes more and more bilingual with Spanish and English becoming the two languages, we have a tendency to resist accepting the fact we are bilingual. Statements I have heard from people with this attitude, "Let them learn English if they want to live in the United States." In Finland, students in elementary school have to learn four foreign languages. They must learn English, Swedish, and Russian. They can choose the fourth, plus they have to know their native language of Finnish, making them able to speak five different languages.

So, as you see we had very little trouble with language in Finland. The older Finn's, could not speak English in most cases, but those educated after 1955 were able to speak the five different languages. In 1955, Finland embarked upon a massive education program to integrate itself into the international market. This program and attitude has improved their economy and life style. When we encountered anyone who could not speak English, all we had to do was to look for a child. In the Russian border town of Virolahti, Finland I met a six-year-old who spoke fluent Russian, German, and English plus Finnish. We were attempting to rent a camper cabin and needed help as the owner of the campground was our age and did not speak English. The child was standing near-by with a USA tee shirt on and when I pointed to his tee shirt and said, "We are from the USA," he said, "I know, I speak English. Would you like for me to help you rent a cabin for the night?" "Yes!" "What other languages do you speak?" "Oh! I speak Russian and German but I still have trouble with my Finnish." We later found out his parents taught at the university in Saint Petersburg, Russia. He rented the cabin for us. His English was better and clearer than a lot of six-year old's I have met here at home.

We mainly stayed in camper villages and in camper cabins. These cabins were small and always came with a trip to the sauna and a free breakfast in the morning. They were cheaper and since the Euro was about 1.25 to 1 US, we had to search for ways to save in order to stay the two plus months we were in Finland. The cost of the hotels in Finland was all above 100 euro or 125 US. We did stay in a few of the spa hotels, just to pamper ourselves after a week in the small cabins. We always carry a tent and sleeping bags just in case we cannot find a hotel, B&B, or camper cabin. This year we did not have to camp as we were able to find a place to stay each night.

A couple times we stayed in museum villages, in buildings filled with antiques and had to use a wood fired sauna on those occasions.

We spent three days in Helsinki taking in the sights and sounds of the city before heading west along the Bay of Finland. As we rode into the city we spotted a large sail boat. I stopped to photograph the boat and discovered she was from the Cayman Islands. It was 130 feet long with a mast standing 155 feet tall and named Cortesa V. As I took the photos of the boat, a member of the crew came over to talk to us (we had on bicycle jerseys from the USA) and wanted to know where we were cycling. I asked her where she was from and she stated, "Oh a place in the US you probable never heard of, Hayward, Wisconsin." "Oh yes!" "The home of the Fresh Water Fish Hall of Fame, the World Lumberjack Championship, and the largest cross-country ski race in the USA, we know where Hayward is located." Then she said, "How?" I said, "We rode across the USA in 1999 and passed through Hayward." She was surprised. After quite a visit we departed Helsinki for the ride of a life-time around the perimeter of Finland.

After a couple days of riding we arrived in the southern-most city in Finland, Hanko. Hanko was controlled by the Russians until the late 1960's and served as a resort town for the Russians. The town is full of period homes of the ginger bread style with beautiful woodwork and carvings. They are now all B&B's and Hanko is a resort town for everyone. From Hanko we caught a foot ferry to the city of Turku and arrived in the middle of a rock festival. "Rolling on the Wharf" plenty of Lapin Kolta, (beer), the Anheuser-Busch of the north, and our first experience with the Finn's passion for drinking. After a couple nights of "Rocking on the Wharf" we caught a ferry to the Åland Islands (pronounced OOOland Islands). The Islands are Finnish but they have their own government and postal system. Also the people speak Swedish and it is difficult to get them to admit they can understand Finnish, so when in Rome do as the Romans, we spoke the few Swedish words we knew and saved our Finnish words for the mainland of Finland.

We arrived in Marichamn, Åland Island, after a full day on the ferry, a Viking Line. We checked with the tourist information office for a place to stay and they found us a room at the Solhem B&B, where we would be for three nights. Also staying at the B&B was a large group of artists from Sweden. Of course, we introduced ourselves and made friends with a couple, Lucis and Sylvia Dahlberg. We remained in contact with them until Christmas of 2019, when we did not receive a card. Our card was not returned. We do not know what has happened to them, but we have a beautiful line drawing by Lucis and a wonderful watercolor by Sylvia of a robin on hand-made paper, both are hanging in our home.

There are over 3,000 islands in the archipelago of the Åland Islands. As we rode the ferry from one island to the next we also had to find places to stay, such as in farm cabins for migrant workers, which worked out to be as nice as the cabins in the camper villages we had been staying in while in Finland. Once we were waiting for the ferry when an old LST (landing ship tanks) from WWII arrived and we were sure this was our ferry. As we began to push our bicycles toward the ferry the captain said, "I don't think this is the ferry you want to take, as I won't be back here for two months." We laughed, thanked him, and we waited for the real ferry to come along. We continued to island hop and after four days arrived back on the mainland. At this point we had reached the western border of Finland along the Bay of Bothnia.

We resumed our trek north toward our goal of the Arctic Circle. On our way, we had a great welcome in the city of

Uusikaupunki, home of the Saab automobile. We took time to visit the Saab Museum. The people there discovered we were from the USA and invited us to go for a ride in one of "Henry's" Fords, a 1929 Ford. They rolled it off the museum floor, hand cranked the motor, and drove us through the city of Uusikaupunki, with the ugga horn blowing as we rode along waving to everyone as we passed. The sight brought out a crowd just as it would here in America and with the same response, a wave as we passed. How many museums in America would roll a 1929 Ford off the floor and give a stranger a ride around town?

Several days later as we were riding on an unpaved country road, we met a lady on a bicycle. Just as she was approaching Ann, she began to shout. "HIRVI! HIRVI! HIRVI!" It sounded as if she was shouting HORRIBLE! HORRIBLE! HORRIBLE! As she approached me I stopped and asked, "Do you speak English?" She stopped, calmed down and said, "Why, of course, do you need some instructions?" "Why are you so excited and what are you shouting about?" She again became overly excited and said. "Oh!" "The hirvi it was coming out in the road, about where your wife is now." "The hirvi, what is a hirvi?" "You know the big animal, the hirvi. It was coming out on the road." "Yes," "But what is a hirvi?" Then she made a motion with her hands as if it had antlers, and I asked. "A moose?" She said "I don't know moose." So I took out my trusty Finnish-English English-Finnish Dictionary and looked up moose. There it was moose-hirvi, so a moose had frightened her and she had frightened the moose. All the time we had ridden in Finland and seen signs warning us of moose crossings and the day a moose was crossing, he was frightened off by a very frightened Finn.

Our next wonderful experience came in the city of Vaasa on June 21, the celebration of the Summer Solstice. This was our first full day of daylight and would last until July 12, before the sun dropped below the horizon again. We thought they had set Finland on fire, for as far as we could see around the shore of the Bay of Bothnia, we saw bon fires. We stayed in a spa hotel in Vaasa and celebrated with the local's and many hotel guests, as we danced the "night away" so to speak. The band played all day or night which ever and we danced and watched the Finn's drink and drink and drink for they do love to drink. As one young Finn told us "What more would a young man want than to sky dive all day and party all night?" They do know how to party and we were no match, so sometime in the early morning hours we gave up and attempted to close out the sun and sleep. The party was still going when we came down for breakfast.

On July 3, 2003, we arrived in the city of Rovaniemi, just eight kilometers south of the Arctic Circle. We decided to wait until the next day to cross the line to become a couple of "Blue Noses" from Germantown, Tennessee. On July 4, 2003, we rode our bicycles across the Arctic Circle and became a "Blue Nose." At this point we had ridden 1,096 miles from Helsinki. That night we rented golf clubs and played nine holes of mid-night golf. We rode our bicycles everywhere we went in Finland, even to play mid-night golf.

We departed Rovaniemi in a rain storm heading toward the Russian border and then turned south along the border heading to the Gulf of Finland. We had tickets waiting in Savonlinna for the Finnish Opera "Juha." "Juha" is a three-act opera by Aarre Merikanto, with a Finnish libretto by Aino Ackté based on the 1911 novel of the same name by Juhani Aho. It was sung in Finnish with English and Swedish sub-titles. The opera was performed in the Olavinlinna Castle in the middle of the river in Savonlinna. Now one has to understand that the Finn's obey the law 120% not 100% but really 120%. Our seats were on row six and we thought it would be perfect, not so, the row curved around the stage. We were just two seats from the wall of the castle and could not read the sub-titles. To our right and in the middle of the row were five seats open, and since they were open, we asked everyone to move over five seats, no way, they would not break the law. Well, being from the USA and knowing we would not be shot for moving, we began to attempt to move to the open seats, when the Finn's saw we were serious about moving, everyone shifted over the five seats and we could read the sub-titles. We enjoyed the opera and the people around us were excited that we had all moved!

During the intermission the conversation was on our bicycling around Finland and where to next. When I told the man next to us we would ride through Imatra, he asked, "Will you see the rabbits when you are in Imatra?" "What rabbits?" "Oh! You must see the rabbits in Imatra." "Are they in the zoo?" "Zoo, no they do not have rabbits in the zoo. They release the rabbits every day at 1700 (5 P.M.) and you must see them for they are very large rabbits." "Well we saw three large Arctic Hare on the west coast of Finland. How large can these rabbits be?" "Why are you talking about hare?" "You keep telling me about the large rabbits in Imatra." "Not rabbits, rabbits, you know the flume." "Oh!" Rapids, not rabbits." "Yes, you must see the rapids." We knew of the rapids from reading about Imatra but to hear the word spoken with an accent that made it sound like rabbits it became a difficult conversation. We all laughed after we figured out the difference.

Yes, we saw the rapids. Every day at 1700 (5 pm) they open the gates on the dam in Imatra for twenty minutes. To the sound of Jean Sibelius's music, the rapids roar through the canyon. You see, in 1912 the founding fathers built a beautiful art deco hotel on the top of the canyon overlooking the rapids, but in 1924 they decided to dam up the river for free electricity. The people stopped coming to the hotel and business dried up. The owners came up with another idea, free electricity and hotel customers, too. They would open the flood gates every day and people would come to see the rapids.

From Imatra, we continued south to the Gulf of Finland and turned west to Helsinki. When we left Vaalimaa heading west, we had planned to ride all day to reach Kotka by night but as we rode out of town we met a group of bicyclists from Switzerland. They gave us the Finnish hello, "HAY." In the Finnish language hay is hello and hay hay is goodbye. But we responded with, "hello." They all stopped and in unison shouted "They're Americans." Then they made the sign of the cross on their chests, bowed, and then the leader spoke. "It says in the good book that the day you meet an American on a loaded touring bicycle, that all the prophecies in the good book will come true. Surely today all the prophecies will come true as we have met two Americans on loaded touring bikes." We all laughed and I asked, "Where are you heading." The response was "Russia." I asked how they got a visa to bicycle in Russia since we had explored the possibility and could not get a visa to bicycle in Russia, and stated we were going on a tour from Helsinki. "I knew it. The prophecies will not come true, they are taking a bus to Russia." "Oh!" "Come with us we will get you across the border and you can see what Russia is really like." We thanked them, but decided to continue to Helsinki, where we caught the train to Saint Petersburg for six days, and yes, we were on a tour bus in Saint Petersburg.

Just twelve kilometers further down the road we saw a sign for an agricultural college, turned off the bicycle route and stopped in for lunch. When we had tasted the food and saw the living accommodations, we decided to stay overnight. Since we had most of the day left, the lady who showed us to our room told us about a swimming hole in the Gulf of Finland that belonged to the college. We dressed in our swim clothes and headed off on our bicycles to the Gulf for a swim. The Gulf of Finland is so shallow one can wade forever and not get over their heads. So, with the shallow water and a warm sun the water was warm enough to swim in and not freeze. We had been swimming for a short time when a lady walked out to the end of the pier looked down at us and said, "May I ask you a question?" "Of course." "May we let our DUCKS go for a swim?" "Why of course." "Now I must warn you they are very large DUCKS." "Great, we would love to see your large DUCKS." "Some people are afraid of large DUCKS and I wanted to be sure it was alright before I let them go for a swim." Then she walked off up the hill and opened the back of her Volvo to release the large DUCKS. Ann looked at me and asked, "She did say DUCKS?" "Yes she said DUCKS." "Look!" Out of the back of the Volvo came a Great Dane and a black Labrador, not DUCKS but two very large DOGS. The Finnish language and English sometimes conflict with each other, as we had already learned.

From the Agricultural College, we returned to Helsinki and caught a ferry across to Estonia. We landed in Tallinn, in the old city, and toured that part of Tallinn. That evening we had dinner in an open-air square and met the ferryboat captain. We began to talk about how shallow the Gulf of Finland is as we had been swimming in it at the Agricultural College. The Captain began to laugh and stated, "If you can see land, it is too shallow for the ferry. We have to watch and be sure we are in the channel." We also talked about riding in Estonia and he recommended riding to Haapsalu, as it is a spa town offering mud baths. Mud baths are a "come on" for us as we had had mud baths at Dr. Wilkinson's in Calistoga, California and enjoyed them, so why not ride to Haapsalu for a mud bath.

We began to explore the route and found it to be too far for a one-day ride, so we had to find a place to stay in between and settled on Paldiski, about half way to Haapsalu. As we rode along toward Paldiski we met a lot of people. When they asked where we were headed and we told them Paldiski, their response was, "You do not want to go there, it is a bad town." "What do you mean it is a bad town?" Their only answer was "It is a bad town." We found that Paldiski was a closed town during the occupation of Estonia by Russia. We also discovered it had been the headquarters for the Russian Nuclear Navy, and a college for the Russian Navy, but now they were gone. A widow and her son had opened a B&B in the old officers' quarters. So why not go to Paldiski for the night?

As we entered the town of Paldiski, it appeared to have been bombed. The windows and roofs of the buildings were blown out and off and the weeds and grass were very deep around these large dormitory type buildings. Ann began to complain about being in Paldiski. There just did not appear to be much left of the town. But, we found the B&B and they made it worth riding to Paldiski for the night. The next morning the heat from a summer heat wave had hit Estonia and we had a long all-day ride to Haapsalu. I stopped on our way out of town to photograph the bombed-out buildings and Ann said, "Let's get out of here, this is depressing." No sooner had she finished her statement when a man rode up on his bicycle and asked her where she was from, "Memphis, TN, USA." He reached into the backpack on his bicycle and pulled out a bouquet of wild flowers, and said, "Welcome to my country." Ann began to smile and thanked him as he had made her day in Paldiski. I finished my photo shoot, and we headed to Haapsalu.

As I stated earlier, a heat wave had hit and so had the warm rains of July. A strong shower hit just as we passed a bus stop, a covered station, with just enough room to pull the bicycles and ourselves out of the rain. This was out in the middle of a forest and it appeared there was no reason for the bus stop in the first place. Out of the woods people appeared in droves, all with buckets of mushrooms and blue berries. The shoving began, first the bicycles, then among themselves, so we climbed behind the seat, held our ground, and stayed dry.

The day was long and really hot, and Ann began to have a hard time with the heat. When we arrived in Haapsalu she began to throw up and became very sick. We looked around for a hospital, and discovered one. We locked the bicycles outside and went into the hospital. Not so fast, we were marched out to the entry, shoe covers were provided and now we could come inside. We explained that Ann had heat exhaustion and needed help. She was taken to a room, examined and given two iv's and pain medicine, and told they would keep her overnight. Then the doctor turned to me and said, "Since you have been with her, I suggest we place you in the other bed for observation." Then to Ann he asked, "Where in the states are you from?" "Memphis, TN," "What!" "This heat should not bother you." Ann then asked, "What do you know about the heat in Memphis?" "I graduated from UT Memphis." What a small world we really live in! The next day, we checked out of the hospital and it cost a total of 108 Kroons, which converted to $8.20, that is correct, eight dollars and twenty cents. I told Ann she had to get sick each night we were in Estonia. Also the doctor would not allow Ann to have a full mud bath, only from the waist down, I had the full treatment. We caught the bus back to Tallinn and arrived in the middle of a modern city. We were lost, as we only knew the Old Town, finally to the ferry dock and back to Finland.

In two months and five days we rode 2,229 miles and visited Sweden, Norway, Russia, Estonia and Finland. Most of our time was in Finland and most of the bicycling was along safe bicycle paths. Would we do it again? Just give us a chance. Bicycling has introduced us to many wonderful people. We are still amazed when someone says, "You look so honest, why don't you come stay with us." This has happened so many times, in the USA, The Netherlands, Belgium, France, Ireland and now in Finland. This happened in Kansas and Missouri, when we needed a place to lay our heads and all the hotels were full and the campground looked like a city dump. But people came along and rescued us. Before 9/11 we felt that "the world was our oyster," and all we had to do was enjoy the beauty of it all, but now we look more closely at our final destinations as we investigate our next bicycle ride. Come join the fun!!! Travel by bicycle, it is great.

2004 From Quebec City to St. John's, Newfoundland

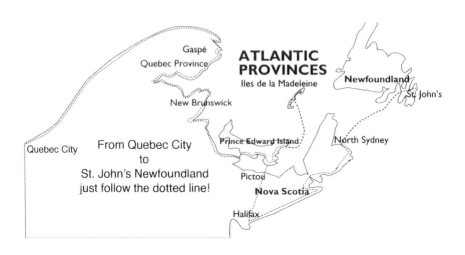

June 13, 2004

This would be our second time since 9-11 to fly but our first experience with airlines since all the travel check points were put in and it was pure HELL! Our oyster was gone! Last year the airlines furnished boxes for our bicycles. This year the cost per bicycle went from free to $140.00 per bicycle, along with the hassle over the boxes for the panniers. We were put on hold for about an hour while everything was checked. During this time six ladies were moved ahead of us in the line, and they must have had metal all over their bodies for each time they walked through the metal detector, they had to return for another check and remove more metal, and try to pass through again. Finally, they had found enough metal to melt down and rebuild a ship, and they were then passed through. We walked through without a beep, and were on our way to the B Concourse to fly to Quebec City. When packing the panniers, the sleeping bags were in a compression bag and therefore were very small. When we began to unpack in Canada, the sleeping bags had been opened and the person checking the contents of the package could not repack them, so we had another thing to redo before heading out of the airport in Quebec City.

First to come through the oversize luggage chute were our bicycles and second, one by one, the boxes containing our panniers. We stood patiently waiting and wondering if everything was on the plane, yes everything arrived and the unpacking and assembling the bicycles began, all was well. We were under the watchful eyes of two border guards, and with only seven people on the plane from Detroit, it had been easy to check into Canada, but rebuilding a bicycle in the luggage room was not something one of the guards enjoyed, the other was helping, so we could be on our way into Quebec City.

Quebec City is one of those very friendly cities to bicyclists, with bike paths out of the airport and most of the way to Old Town. I asked one of the border guards about the address to the B&B and he called the number just to be told our reservations had been canceled as our room had been given to a regular. This had happened in Ireland but not Canada, oh, yes even in Canada. The border guard also wanted to help us find another place to stay and knew about another B&B the Auz Franciscains run by Lorraine Rousseau, yes she had room. The guard gave us directions and off we rode into the city. When we turned the corner of the street to approach the B&B, Lorraine was standing on the porch and began to wave us on to the B&B. We were welcomed by her and her husband Victor, who was from Chili, and was also the cook for breakfast in the morning.

June 14, 2004

I would list the breakfast, but the list would fill a couple pages. Then we had to find the Mountain Equipment Co-Op to buy GAZ for our camp stove, which we had purchased in Europe. It burned a special canister of gas called GAZ, and it was the only canister which would fit. Since the store did not open until 9:00 a.m., we had time to kill and did so in a coffee shop. As we waited, it began to rain, little by little it would rain, stop, rain again and then appear as if the sun was coming out, and then rain.

Since we had been in Quebec City many times and wanted to get on the road around the Gaspé Peninsula, Ann made a command decision. We would catch the ferry over to Lewis and see how the weather was after the ferry ride. Around 1:00 p.m. we decided to ride 33 miles to Montmagny. Upon arriving in town we checked into the Wig-Wam Motel. As soon as we walked into the room I began to look for Norman Bates, as it was like walking into the Bates Motel. Then we discovered a

B&B just around the corner, but now we are stuck in the Bates Motel, cheap, clean, but rustic.

June 15, 2004

This was a dry day, the rain was out of our way and we felt free to ride all day, so we rode to La Pocatière and again checked into a motel before looking around. La Pocatière is the home of an agricultural college and we could have taken a room at the college with dinner, and breakfast at the college all fresh from their gardens. We had the wind at our backs all day. We met a couple who had started in St John's, Newfoundland. They had been riding into the wind all the way. He had chosen the route and she had plenty to say about their decision to ride east to west. They had also ridden across the USA twice.

June 16, 2004

With the wind at our backs and riding 20 mph we made great time to Kamouraska. It was the most attractive town so far on this trip. We also found a great Auberge, shops, and colorful houses all overlooking the St. Lawrence River. The River is controlled by the tide, and when the tide is out people living on the off-islands walk across the salt marshes back home. When the tide comes back in, there is a ferry to the islands. This gave us plenty of people watching!

June 17, 2004

The night of June 16, was almost perfect. As we left Kamouraska, we were told that St. Simon had an auberge, with a great host, wonderful dinner and breakfast and a quiet room. We thought it could not get any better after yesterday, wrong, another auberge with a gourmet chef and dinner presented fit for a queen (Queen Ann)! We were in the town of St. Simon, and dinner was served. Ann started with sea snails, me, I had the shrimp cocktail, second, a green salad for each, for the main course, Ann had lamb and I had the lapin (rabbit). For dessert Ann had rhubarb pie, I had the home-made cheese cake with blueberry sauce. In the states, we would be looking at a $200.00 dinner, here in Canada, a third of the price, $60.00 Canadian and that included our room and breakfast and that was before the adjustment for the exchange rate. Breakfast was just as good and we were very slow in getting started on our ride.

The owner of the auberge, advised us to go inland to avoid the heavy traffic on the main highway. We took his advice, but it was a climb inland and the hills began to take their toll. We ended up pushing up many of them. We were riding Highway 132, and climbing steep hills, little traffic, but pushing a lot as the hills become steeper. Along the way we passed a llama farm with the field full of children out on a day trip, then into St Mathiew and headed east. The hills were not as steep, and we were riding more. When we arrived in St Fabien we were surprised to see one of our hosts from St Simon, Jacque. He wanted to know how we had enjoyed the quiet of Highway 132. "Yes great," and then more advice for our ride around the Gaspe, "Ride the bicycle trail through Pac de Bic." Bad advice! The trail was in poor condition with a lot of loose gravel and unpaved parts to the trail. We climbed back to 132 and found a place where we could cook, and wash the bicycles. My cooking, all I had to do was boil water, and we had one of our freeze-dried dinners.

June 19, 2004

Instant oatmeal for breakfast and we were off ahead of a rain storm but with a great tailwind. Along the way we stopped in a Chinese restaurant for lunch, and to get out of the rain. We had sunshine after lunch. When we began to look for a place to stay the night we spotted a man putting a sign in his yard for a B&B and asked if he was open, "I am now, you will be our first customers. We checked in just ahead of the rain and enjoyed meeting Jean Piesee and his wife.

June 20, 2004

We started our day with a 5 km. ride to the Reford Gardens for a tour of the gardens and house before breakfast. After the video of how the house and gardens were saved by the great-grand son of the original owners, we were served breakfast. We started with great coffee, raisin bread, two kinds of Pâté, strawberry and blueberry jams, wild honey and honey from domestic flowers, a different taste, and we were stuffed.

We had a gale force tailwind and a level road along the river at sea level, with only a bump but not a continual climb at any time, then back to sea level. This was wonderful bicycling. Our lunch was in Baie-des-Sables, and we discovered the owner was an artist. She had a beautiful painting of a cat sitting by a door waiting for someone to open the door. We offered to buy the painting but she informed us it was not for sale. Later in the ride when we arrived in Matane, we stopped at the information center looking for an overnight stop, they gave us two places, a hotel and a gite,(a gîte originally meant quite simply a form of shelter). We rode past the hotel and on to the gite. Wow! What a find, the places to stay just get better the further around the Gaspe.

June 21, 2004

Wind was at our backs, sun overhead and a flat highway ahead along the Saint Lawrence Seaway. We were so close to the seaway, only the oncoming lane was between us and water, and the water was less than four feet below the highway. There were signs posted showing waves coming over the roadway. This was one of those days bicyclists dream of and we had found the place, and we were enjoying the day. Later in the day we stopped at a butcher shop in Martre to ask about a place to stay, first, we asked "Do you speak English" "Non" so we said, "Nous avons besoin d'un endroit pour dormir" or in English, we need a place to sleep, and he answered in English, "There's a hotel in Marsoui about five miles ahead." I said, "Merci beaucoup," and we rode off with the butcher laughing. When we arrived at the hotel we were surprised to be welcomed with such a fanfare. The owner and staff were standing in the street waiting for us. Then we discovered the butcher had called the hotel and told them we were on our way and needed a room.

June 22, 2004

A whale! We, spotted a whale. When we stopped for a break, a man from Pennsylvania showed us the whale. He was a Doctor. He was traveling alone by car with his bicycle on the top of his car. "Bonjour, why are you not riding your bicycle?" "What!" "Where did that accent come from?" "Tennessee, Memphis and you?" "With that Bonjour I thought you were locals, I'm from Penn State." He shared his grapes and blueberries with us as we watched the whale.

This was another one of those found days for bicycling, wind at our backs, flat highway with very few rises and falls so we made great headway until the wind changed from the west to the east. This was not a good sign as it was going to rain. We arrived in Sainte-Madeleine-de-la-Rivière and found a hotel overlooking the Saint Lawrence Seaway. We were on top of a hill and the view of the Saint Lawrence Seaway was perfect, so we sat, had a glass of wine and watched the ships in the Seaway.

June 23, 2004

This was a different day, short on miles and long on hills. We had a two-mile climb at 14% grade, long and slow and then climbed a 13% grade followed by a 11% and then a 9% before we reached Grande-Vallée. We were whipped. We hitched a ride the rest of the way to Cloridorme. We tried to pay the driver but he would not take the money, so we gave him our card and invited him to Memphis. When we checked into the hotel, the chef was chopping up lobsters for lobster bisque for dinner that evening. From our window we spotted a school of minke whales playing in the Seaway, and it was cold, overcast and beginning to rain.

June 24, 2004

This would be our first full day off the bicycles since we had arrived in Canada and we needed the day off. We bummed a ride in an SUV from Cloridorme to Gaspé with Max. He drove too fast, tailgated cars, but stopped at every overlook along the way. He also stopped at all the points of interest. Otherwise we would have missed the lighthouse and wireless station where Guglielmo Marconi sent the first wireless telegraphy across the Atlantic. When we arrived at the end of our ride, Max dropped us off in a very large park at the tip of the Gaspé at the Adam Hotel. Lunch was very expensive, $50.00 after tip and taxes. Also Max had charged us $20.00 each for the ride along with hauling our bicycles. This was a very expensive day. That afternoon we watched two men cleaning and weighing a couple Atlantic Salmon, each about 25 pounds. We also met a couple from Nova Scotia and another from Toronto who were fishing for cod, but had only a catch and release permit. No bicycling today but a much needed rest, as well as missing the many climbs.

June 25, 2004

Today we rode form Gaspé to Douglastown and entered New Brunswick, just 14 kilometers, a little over 10 miles. We were racing against a rainstorm. A young man and his son watched as we entered Douglastown and asked if we needed information. We explained we needed to find a place to stay and also to get out of the on-coming rain. He told us about a youth hostel, and I asked if he had ever stayed in a youth hostel? "No" "We have." Then he explained that this one was new and well kept. So we rode on to the post office and asked about a place to stay, same answer, so we stopped at the youth hostel. Wow! It was new, it was clean, it was quiet, and we could wash our clothes, wash our bicycles, have lunch, dinner, and a community breakfast. Yes! We stayed at this youth hostel!

June 26, 2004

The ride today took us into the town of Percé. With the help of two brothers our knees were saved from a long 17% grade and then a second time when we took a wrong turn which would have us back over the same mountain we had just avoided. We arrived in Percé around 3:00 p.m. and discovered a wonderful Gite and settled in after a great day of bicycling.

Dinner was in a restaurant overlooking the bay and Percé Rock. We were having mussels for the first time on this trip. We were watching Northern Gannets diving for anchovies. The sky was white with these large birds and the water was white foam from their dives from high in the sky. Wave after wave of Northern Gannets filled the sky. Later we discovered we could take a tour of Bonaventure Island and see the gannets up close in their nests. Fog played a game of in and out as we watched the birds and Percé Rock appeared and disappeared.

June 27, 2004

With the discovery of a trip to Bonaventure Island, we took a side trip out to see the Northern Gannets nesting. We had lots of time to kill, as the tour boat did not leave until 9:30 a.m. and being a shy couple, we met two couples from France. The first couple lived in the Dordogne Region, and were very impressed that we had ridden our bicycles through the area. Their English was short, and of course our French was also, but we did communicate with each other. Then we met a couple from Paris who had no English until the husband let a couple English words slip out, and we knew they were a couple of asses. We moved on to board the boat for our trip to see the nests of 250,000 Northern Gannets.

The noise from the birds calling to each other from the ones on their nests to the ones flying was so loud we could hardly carry on a conversation. Birds, as far as one could see were sitting on nests and the sky was full of birds darting back and forth overhead. I asked the guide, "Do they ever collide?" Just about that time two hit head on, fell to the ground rolled around, staggered to their feet and continued this until they were able to fly off to wherever they fly. The odor was strong from bird poop. We were left to do our own tour, so we did what we usually do, we took a hike. The rain stopped us short of walking all the way around the island. That evening we returned to the same wonderful restaurant as the night before for more mussels and to watch the birds perform their dives. We learned that they dive about 30 feet deep to feed on anchovies.

June 28, 2004

It was election day in Canada, and the locals could drink, not like Mexico, where the locals cannot drink on election day. The Blue Party is the party of choice for Quebec Province. This was according to the owner of the Auberge. He then told a story about the local Priest on the Sunday before the election who had reminded his parishioners that, "The sky is blue and that is where heaven is located." "Red is hell!" " So when you vote think of heaven." The Red Party won, with the Blue Party coming in second.

This was the hardest day of riding to date, with a 30-mph head wind we made the 28 miles to Chandler and died. We checked into the Motel St. Laurent. Dinner was great as we had lobster. When we were in Percé we met Hebert, photographing the gannets and now we were in Chandler and so was Hebert. He had taken us under his wing and now we were headed to the Marina Restaurant. Since he knew the owners, we were seated on the second floor overlooking the harbor so we could watch the Northern Gannets diving for a second evening.

As we ate dinner it began to rain, and just outside the harbor a beautiful rainbow formed. We could see the ends and the bow was over the entrance of the harbor, no camera, no photo, and then a second rainbow formed in front of the first, and we watched as they moved out to sea and disappeared. The rain stopped, the sun returned and the gulls began to fly in long white lines just a few feet above the water. Thanks to Hebert we had a wonderful evening of laughs and a super dinner.

June 29, 2004

Today we wanted to ride to Bonaventure, a distance of 56 miles. We started out with a little head wind and a level ride, but things change in Canada and so did the wind and terrain. As the wind increased it became colder so we stopped in a small diner (a "casse-croûte") for coffee and toast. The weather was getting worse and we still had a long ride ahead if we were to reach Bonaventure. By noon we were in Saint-Godefroi, and stopped at the marina for fish soup with coffee and left with 25 miles to ride before evening. As we departed Saint-Godefroi the land flattened and the wind slowed, and we made it to Bonaventure by 4:30 p.m., checked into an auberge, showered, rested and now we sat on the porch with a glass of wine. The owner had joined us. He was in shorts, bare feet and needed a haircut. He knew English and had promised me pan seared smelts, better than we had had in Finland, hard to believe, but yes, it was better, no heads, and served on a bed of rice, a salad and a wonderful meal. We walked to the pier to people watch as it seemed everyone in Bonaventure was fishing. The only person with English was a 90-year-old who said he had sold his canoe to purchase his fishing permit, as a permit to fish for salmon was very expensive. As we stood around, a lady caught a flounder about the size of a small hand, then a second and the fuss began about the size of the fish with everyone joining in to brag about the size of their fish, with many laughs.

June 30, 2004

The Canadians have a breakfast I really enjoy, eggs and baked beans. So, after breakfast we again had to decide to ride in a rain suit or stop over to let the rain pass, we rode. In New Richmond we ducked onto the porch of a Jehovah's Witnesses church to get out of a shower, and stay dry. Now we have to deal with the splatters from passing automobiles as we ride toward Carleton-sur-Mer. We checked into a Gite with a view overlooking the bay. Across the bay was New Brunswick. This would be our last day in Quebec Province. On our way we met a group of cyclists with a sag truck and since tomorrow would be Canada Day, we asked if this is part of "Canada Day" Celebration, "No way, we do not celebrate Canada Day in Quebec Province." Also since we were from the USA they let us know how much they hated President Bush. We did not answer, but soon found we were in the wrong Province on the wrong day.

July 1, 2004

After seventeen days of riding in Quebec Province, we entered New Brunswick Province. We decided to visit the Parc national de Miguasha and dig for fossils. It took a couple long climbs to reach the Park, but we were excited to look for fossils. We had a wonderful guide in the park and she split open a couple of rocks that we thought might contain fossils but no luck.

Lunch in the park and then to highway number 132 again, but this time it was under repair, gravel, loose and slippery. Some pushing and some riding but we had to share the pot holes with the traffic. When we came to the Matapedia River we walked our bicycles across the bridge into Campbellton. Of course, first to the tourist information center, to find a B&B. That evening we had a wonderful salmon dinner at the local Curling Club, which included fiddle head ferns as a side dish. English was spoken and we felt very welcome.

July 2, 2004

Today we had a very short ride into Dalhousie before the rain started in buckets, not drops, but there was no way we could ride, so we looked for a place to stay and discovered there was only one place in Dalhousie, the Best Western and then we discovered it was booked solid. I asked if we waited at the pizza place and there was a cancelation would she come tell us about the opening. "These rooms have been booked for a year, there is no chance of a cancelation." Just then the phone rang and I listened as the other person on the phone cancelled their reservation. Bingo! We had a room but it was on the third floor and a smoking room. Ok! We do not smoke and we took the room, $99.00 for one night. We have to save, so, we bought cheese, olives, wine and cookies for dinner. We also had all afternoon so, a shower, nap, and napped again. We had instant oatmeal for breakfast. We were off toward Bathurst, in the fog. We prayed that our lights would be enough to save us from the traffic. We made it into Bathurst and found a B&B.

July 4, 2004

"Independence Day" Ours's not Canada's

Fog and more fog, so we waited until we were sure it was safe to ride on the highway. We departed Bathurst on highway 134, and then to Trans-Canada Highway 11. After a few miles we were told about a very scenic bicycle path but, after three miles it turned into the path from HELL, large rocks, loose rocks and broken pavement and no way to ride on such a trail. We began to look for any way to return to a paved highway. We discovered a trail through the woods that led us back to Trans-Canada Highway 11 and back on a surface we could ride for the rest of the day. We stopped in Pokemouche. We discovered the Landry Motel and our welcome was more than we expected, Laverine Landry, the owner not only welcomed us, she drove us to a fish market for dinner. Yes! We had mussels and clam chowder for dinner. Wow! What a wonderful ending to a long day of traveling on a bicycle and a great way to end the 4th of July, 2004.

July 5, 2004

Fog was still following us around New Brunswick and the wind was in our faces. After about five miles we ran into a wall of traffic, but we were on bicycles, so we continued as there was no traffic coming toward us, we knew it had to be an accident, but now we came to a stop, A HOUSE, sat across the road, so we were delayed about an hour along with all the traffic we had passed earlier. During our waiting time two more bicyclists joined up with us and we found that they had started in Vancouver and were also heading to St. John's, our finishing point, we hoped. Once we passed the house, we stopped for lunch along with the riders heading to St. John's. When we headed out again the wind had really come up and the going was slowed to a stand-still. Our fellow bicyclists were stronger and rode on, saying they would see us in St. John's.

We made it to Neguac and the visitor center to search for a place for the night. Not only did we find a place to stay but a lady who taught us how to make bread in a clay oven in her back yard. We also had dinner with fresh baked bread and a bottle of wine. Ann would suffer in the morning but tonight we were very happy. That night we slept with the door open as the room was not air conditioned. We listened to rain, traffic noise, and burglars who were stealing our bicycles, well at least Ann heard them, and of course I was the one who had to stop the burglars which I could not find.

July 6, 2004

We checked out late and headed to Miramichi, Ann was suffering from a head ache, hang over and threating to throw-up, so we delayed our start until she was able to ride. We had a reservation at the Sunny Side B&B in Miramichi, and again we were stuck on the Trans-Canada Highway with large trucks. One of the trucks was a low-boy carrying lobster boats. As we stopped for coffee it pulled into the parking lot and we were told lobster season was over and all lobster boats had to be pulled out of the water and that we would be seeing a lot of him if we continued along the shoreline. We did, each day he would pass us a couple or more times each day, waved, blow his horn and gave us the thumbs up as he passed.

As we arrived in Miramichi we were faced with a bridge over the Miramichi River that looked awesome so we walked our bicycles across the bridge. As we began to look for Henderson Street a local stopped us and asked if we were looking for the B&B. Yes! "You're almost there just two blocks, then right two more blocks and it is on your left just past the recreation center." Thanks, and we rode along on our way to the B&B, thinking of the many people who had helped us find our way, find a place to stay and a place to eat, just a few ways the locals came to our aid. We were blessed!

July 7, 2004

We were out by 8:30, with a great tail-wind and riding about 14 mph on our way to the Parc national Kouchibouguac. It was a beautiful forest and we were loving the ride, but then, we had a surprise, a real big surprise, a bear. Not just any bear but the largest black bear we had ever seen anywhere. It was standing in the middle of the road, and I think it was about 12 or 14 feet tall. We stopped with the bear about 100 yards ahead and began to wonder "what if" as the bear stood sniffing the air and our smell was in the air. Then the low-boy with a lobster boat came lumbering up beside us and the bear ran off the road into the woods. The driver's passenger rolled down the window on the truck and said, "I hate to tell you this but bicyclists are their favorite food." We all began to laugh and the truck moved on and we did also. That was the only bear we spotted on this trip.

That evening we had to camp in the Kouchibouguac forest at the Côte-à-Fabien campground, a primitive campground. It was quiet, no showers, a deep hole toilet, no lights, and no noise. WRONG! As always with primitive campgrounds, there was always a loud mouth drunk who thinks everyone should know he is present. This went on until 2:30 a.m. before they dropped off to sleep or passed out from drinking and we went to sleep.

July 8, 2004

Since we got up early, we were also able to hold reveille, which made us feel better for missing sleep but of course caused some stress by having to face the drunks. We had our usual instant oatmeal and instant coffee and we were off to Richibucto. We were looking for a place to stay in Cap-Lumière and found the Arcadian B&B. It was run by Linda Daigle. She was cooking dinner and invited us to join her, of course for a price, but where can you get dinner and a room for $55.00 Canadian, about $45.00 US? We were enjoying the exchange rate.

July 9, 2004

It had rained all night and everything was wet, the streets were so wet we would have rooster tails when we started our ride. The start of the day was delayed but we had a great breakfast and it was even better than dinner. Our landlady had picked wild strawberries for our oatmeal, baked fresh bread, sliced and toasted with plenty of jam. After all that and instructions not to pass the Oliver Soap Factory, we were off. The stop was a joke, the young lady giving the talk was ok but not worth the time wasted on the stop. Ann bought soap as a present for the girls back home and we are off again.

We stopped in Shediac for the night and what a surprise! The Lobster Festival was taking place. So finding a place to stay took us to Chez Morgan Place, a B&B. We took the last room, a walk-up to the third floor with four rooms and the two bathrooms were on the ground level. The place was packed and even had a barber chair on the front porch, with hair on the floor. We walked to the festival.

Like any local festival, the venders were set up, selling their goods and of course there was a large stage for entertainment. The first performers come on stage in the form of a stomp dance, and then a young boy on a guitar much larger than he. So the entertainment was local and we moved on to the food tent.

This turned out to be the smartest thing we did while in Shediac. Two lobsters, potato salad, cole slaw and two beers, all for $45.00 Canadian, about $35.00 US. The exchange rate in 2004 was the best since our ride there in the early 90's. As we were eating the sky opened up and a rain storm descended on Shediac, lightning and thunder roaring overhead. We were inside a tent and in came the rest of the people at the festival. We held our seats and Gary Knott joined us, and ordered three beers. We thanked him and talked while the lightening flashed. The festival broke up during the rain storm. When we got a break in the weather, Ann and I decided to make a run, or a fast walk, back to the B&B and made it about half way before the rain hit again. We ducked into a gas station, called a cab and returned to the B&B.

The next morning for breakfast we were given one slice of Texas toast, stuffed with banana and fried on top of the stove. Ok! It wasn't that bad but we had had the same thing a couple of days before with this story. "This is an old family recipe. It has been in the family for years." And now we got the same story about the stuffed banana bread for breakfast.

July 10, 2004

There was one thing for sure. We were leaving Shediac and going south, as this was surely a death trap and a health hazard called a B&B. We left in the rain and headed for the Confederation Bridge to cross over to Prince Edward Island. The shuttle ran every hour on the hour and we were about thirty minutes early, so we killed time talking to other bicyclists. The Confederation Bridge Bridge is across the Abegweit Passage of the Northumberland Strait linking the province of Prince Edward Island with the province New Brunswick on the mainland. The bridge opened May 31, 1997. The 12.9-kilometre (8 mi) bridge is Canada's longest bridge and it is the world's longest bridge over ice-covered water. The nice thing about Canada is that they furnish a shuttle across the bridge. When it comes to tunnels or long bridges they really support bicycle travel.

The bridge is between Cape Jourimain, New Brunswick and Borden-Carleton, Prince Edward Island. The shuttle dropped us at the information center in Borden-Carleton, so we could find a B&B for the night. The clerk recommended the Bridge View B&B in Cape Traverse. It was a real find, when we discovered that the owner, Grace Harvy, is a Presbyterian and we stated it had been a long summer without going to church. We were invited to join her that Sunday. She drove us to the North Tryon Presbyterian church. This would be our second night with Grace and then Ann became sick during the night, and we took another day off for her to recoup from the cramps and an upset stomach. That was not enough, as during the night I woke up with cramps, throwing up and too sick to travel, so another night with Grace before we headed to Charlottetown. This was our first warm day in weeks, no foul weather clothing, just shorts and bike jerseys.

We took the shoreline road to Charlottetown and found a room for a couple of nights in a Tourist House. We needed our bicycles cleaned and oiled, so we dropped them off before returning to ask about dinner. The owner recommended a Greek place for dinner, great place to eat, but the location of the Tourist House was the noisiest place we stayed on the ride, with loud street talk, motorcycles, and then at 2:00 a.m. a bouncing noise, yes a basketball going down the street, and then a crying child, loud cars, and I could go on and on before we fell asleep out of exhaustion. The next morning we went to Cora's for breakfast, and a waitress with an attitude problem but in the end I felt I had won, no tip.

With another day in Charlottetown, we went for a ride in a Duck, a wonderful experience. Next we went to the bike shop to pick up our bikes which looked just as they had when we dropped them off, much arguing with the owner before we took the bikes. The second night in Charlottetown was much the same as the first and we were pleased to ride out of town toward Morell. We were taking a bus drivers holiday, as we were riding unloaded around the bay and into Cavendish, over the Stanly Bridge and back through the country to Brackley Beach. We were staying in a B&B on a farm, goats, rabbits, ducks, cats, and three sheep dogs. The place was really for children but we were there enjoying soap making, goat milking and duck feeding.

All the travel on Prince Edward Island was taking us to a ferry ride across to the French Islands, Îles de la Madeleine. Dinner that evening was on the ferry, with lots of attention from the other passengers. They asked about our equipment, travels, clothing, our bicycles, and last our age. All of them wanted to do the same someday, always someday. Our stay in the Îles de la Madeleine's was in one B&B with a wonderful hostess. She came to the islands in the spring and spent the summer and returned home to Quebec in early fall. This was truly one of the great finds when it came to B&B's as she was a wonderful hostess, chef and guide. We were directed to the east end of the island to visit the salt mines, and had a guided tour of the mines and the mining operation.

Breakfast each morning was too much, too much to eat, and too much to describe. Jo Ann was our landlady and each morning she and I worked on my French, and laughed. One morning I was up early, made the coffee and sat enjoying the sounds of the gulls, and other birds, watched the sun rise, and prayed for peace on earth for in this place there really was peace on earth. The sand dunes were covered with purple clover and many other flowers making the landscape a blanket of flowers of many colors.

This was truly a place to enjoy island life. Some sections of the island were only French, others only English and others spoke whatever was spoken to them. There were few white houses on the island, mostly blue or yellow but we saw other colors as we rode from end to end on the island.

One day we rode west for five hours with a great tailwind, and along the way a tourist bus passed us many times, and each time I waved and the bus driver and passengers also waved. It paid off as when we turned to return with a strong head wind, we asked for a ride and he loaded our bikes on the bus and saved us from a hard ride into a strong head wind. Bicycling is a nice way to travel most of the time but the wind can make you humble when it is in your face for hours.

    The next morning we took an excursion around the islands on a small boat, visited the sea life, saw a seal colony of about 40 seals. Then the guide took us to a mussels farm, a scallop bed, unloaded a lobster trap and then to shore to a small restaurant for Moules-frites, meaning mussels and French fries. On our way back to the B&B, we stopped by a smoke house and purchased a bag of smoked herring, bought a six-pack of beer and returned to eat fish and drink beer. We would smell like fish for the next week!

    After two days with Jo Ann, we moved to the Le Solei Le Vent or The Sea and Wind Gite. We were welcomed with open arms upon our arrival. Our room was on the second floor and the bath on the ground floor, but after one night we returned to Jo Ann's and now we were enjoying her deck as we waited for dinner.

    The next morning we were heading into the wind to a Tea House in Eloge Du-nord. This area of the islands hosted a sand sculpture contest each year and many of the sculptures were still standing as we rode along the beach. Also, there was a threat of rain in the air, and to get out of the showers, we first ducked into a garden shop and green house, second into a glass blowers shop, then the porch of the International Lions club house, and then to the Tea House for lunch. All the time missing the rain. As I stated, we rode into the wind so our return would be a breeze, not so as we ate lunch, we watched the flags turn from with us to in our faces. OK! We could handle that. That evening Jo Ann had fired up the grill, had steaks for me to cook, baked potatoes for the three of us and a dinner in style for our last night with her. We were moving again in the morning to be closer to the ferry, for tomorrow would be our last night on the island. It was a sad departure from Jo Ann's and the Îles de la Madeleine's.

We were moving to Mur Veille near the ferry terminal. That evening we went to La Maison d'Eva-Anne for dinner, here it was referred to as supper, so we were eating supper on a porch with two families, each with lots of children and a chef trying to please everyone. It was turning into a show and we were the audience with a side table. We enjoyed our meal and watched the last sunset we saw before leaving the Îles de la Madeleine's. Early the next morning we returned to Prince Edward Island.

We arrived at one in the afternoon, found a B&B and made plans to ride hard the next day to catch a ferry over to Nova Scotia. We made it into Pictou for the night. It would take us a couple days to ride from Pictou to Halifax, so we needed a couple places to stay. First we were directed to Bruce Fulton's B&B in Middle Musquodoboit.

The next morning we rolled out of Pictou around 11:00 a.m., heading to Middle Musquodoboit, about 106 kms. away. When we were passing through Stellerton, we were to ride highway 289, but we missed the turn and then realized, we had been here before, in 1995 when we rode around Nova Scotia. We missed the highway then and again now, but luck was on our side this time. We spotted a RCMP car, and asked where highway 289 had disappeared to? He laughed and said "Follow me," he cranked his car, turned on his flashers, and we headed through Stellerton for Mateland. We all broke into laughter at the intersection where he dropped us off on highway 289, which we would ride into Middle Musquodoboit.

When we were a few miles from the B&B, yes the bottom fell out and the rain came down in buckets. We dodged the rain on the porch of a farm house. The owner asked where we were staying and when we stated "Bruce Fulton's B&B," it brought on the hardiest laugh and he said "Big Bruce." When we arrived we knew at once what he meant by "Big Bruce." Bruce Fulton was a shadow of his former self as he had lost over 200 pounds and was down to a mere 650 pounds, down from his all-time high of 850 pounds. He had a stool with wheels on it to roll around his house as he could not walk, his bed had a machine like a block and tackle to lift him into his bed. He had plenty of help, and even served breakfast.

On the 29th of June we rode into Halifax to an over-crowded city just as the tall ships were coming into the harbor. As we rode to the waterfront the Mexican tall ship arrived, followed by the American Eagle, (the training ship for the US Coast Guard), then the Tenacious from the UK, then the Pogoria from Poland followed by the Mercea from Romania. They all stood tall for they are truly the tall ships. We walked aboard the Blue Nose II. It was such a beautiful ship as were all of the tall ships. The harbor was full of ships and the shore line packed with people. Tables and chairs from the local restaurants lined the docks. Ann and I joined several people at a table and of course since we were in bicycle "uniforms," the questions were, where did you come from, Quebec City, and heading for St. Johns, they were in disbelief and more questions followed. Then the question of where are you staying? When we told them we had stayed at Bruce Fulton's B&B, one of the ladies said, "We are from Middle Musquodoboit and Big Bruce was the best dancer in our class in school." Well he does not dance any more as he rolls his body around on a stool, we all began to laugh. She also told us about a place to stay north of Halifax. It was a B&B owned by an English couple and a great place to stay. She was correct, it really was a wonderful place to stay. When you are in Halifax, there are other places to visit, the Citadel and the Public Gardens.

We took the next day off for a trip by bus to Peggy's Cove and to watch the fireworks on the wharf beside the Blue Nose II. We met a couple enjoying the fireworks and of course we talked about our travels and where we would ride to from Halifax. When we left town we rode the ferry across the harbor and then east along the shore and into Musquodoboit Harbor. We rode the shoreline of Nova Scotia all day as we headed northeast to Liscomb. In Liscomb, we stayed at the Sherbrook Village built in the 1870's. We found a B&B named Port Bickenton by the Sea, run by Dolores and Bruce Kaiser. Bruce was in Halifax for treatment for cancer and Dolores was alone. Then Ann made a mistake, she asked, "Do you have the game of Scrabble?" Dolores eyes popped out and out came a professional Scrabble board, letters, and score pad. Then she stated, "Bruce and I play every night." It showed as she played three (3) seven (7) letter words during the game and won by a score of 578 to our 120's. We tucked our tails and went to bed.

We had been riding for six days without a day off and both of us are touchy and cross. We kept thinking maybe tomorrow we could take a day off and just rest. On August 6, that day came, it was raining and we had hills, head wind and more rain. Along the route, we had to ride a ferry. We were in Canada and bicyclists were free, National Parks were free, bridges were free and now ferries were free. By the end of the day we were dead, really dead, so we made plans to take the next day off. Yes we were going to rest. When dinner time came we went to the Rare Bird Pub, we had atmosphere and romance filled our hearts, the evening was great! The next day, we slept in, really slept in late. This turned into a wonderful day off for the two of us and now we felt kind toward each other again. The second evening we borrowed a scrabble game, no other players, just the two of us with Ann winning the first game and I won the second by one point, 301 to 300.

On August 8, we were crossing the Straights of Canso and all the traffic, from Halifax was heading home, also crossing the Straights. We were weaving our way across, when we heard our names, who would know us in Nova Scotia? It turned out that the mother of the couple with whom we had watched fireworks with in Halifax was heading home and was crossing the Straights. She spotted us and wanted to let us know her son and daughter-in-law had told her about us and she wanted to talk to us also about our travels on a bicycle. The three of us went to Papa's Pub for food, beer and entertainment. The group playing at Papa's was from PEI. They were very good, with the lead singer, Lennie Gallant.

The next morning we discovered we were not the only guests staying in the B&B. An idiot, who attempted to pass himself off as a professor of religion, cap on his head, elbows on the table, picking his teeth, and insulting our hostess, a wonderful lady named Erline. Thank God for ladies like her. In hindsight I wish I had come to her defense but it would have just given the idiot more fuel for his rant.

After breakfast, Erline, made us a care package of sandwiches, fruit and muffins. The first 25 kms. we rode on a wide interstate style highway with plenty of traffic. Then as we turned onto Fleur-de-Lis Road, very little traffic and very much through the country. In St. Peters we found a place to stay in the country. We were told we would have to purchase our dinner in St. Peters, so we did along with a bottle of wine.

Oh! Wow! What a discovery! This was a log cabin of the finest. The cabin was located on the end of a point high above St. Esprit Lake with a view on all sides, a long porch across the front and chairs and tables on the porch, a perfect place to eat our dinner and drink the wine we had purchased in St.

Peters. Ann and I were lucky to have the ability to travel by bicycles and reap the joys of all the beauty and wonders of traveling through countries and meeting great people. This was just one of those places, the kind of place with people that make you want to stop and stay longer than just one night. Our breakfast was delivered around 8:00 a.m., a good German breakfast, cold cuts, cheese, coffee and boiled eggs. We were on our own in the log cabin. The breakfast reminded us of our ride in Finland especially the boiled eggs. We loaded our bicycles and made a slow escape from paradise with many regrets that we could not stay longer.

The ride took us over rolling hills with great views of the ocean along the shoreline, with large puffy clouds which cooled us as they blocked the sun. We found a picnic table on the shore of Lake Gabarus just past Fourchu Bay. This was a great day to bicycle and see the beauty of Nova Scotia, thanks to the pleasure of traveling by bicycle. Along the way we met a young Frenchman who told us that our ride to Louisbourg along the Mira River would be even more rewarding than where we had already passed. We would stop in Marion Bridge for the night with another day to reach Louisbourg.

We reached Louisbourg on August 11, after a wonderful day of bicycling, first along the Mira River and then cross country into Louisbourg. Our hosts were surprised that we were traveling by bicycle, in fact they were in awe of our travels. This was a great B&B with wonderful hosts. The first night we were invited to attend a play at the local play-house. The owner of the B&B was the Master of Ceremonies and introduced Ann and me with much fanfare. He talked more about his guests, than the show he was to introduce.

The next day we rode to Fort Louisbourg, a former French fort, and we were challenged at the gate as to what country we were loyal to. Then we were allowed to enter the fort.

There were lots of reenactments going on inside the fort and we spent most of the day at Fort Louisbourg. The rest of the day was just lazy and slow, washing clothes and getting ready to travel in a couple days.

On August 13, the hosts and guests, along with lots of friends loaded into a truck and traveled to the Mira River to go swimming. When in Rome do like the Romans. This was true in our case, when everyone went into the river for a swim we did also. Everyone took off across the river and so did Ann and I, without any thought as to how far we had to swim. When we returned to shore we began to talk about, how stupid we had been to swim without any life guard or life support. A cramp, or just not being able to swim the distance could have been the end of life. We enjoyed the swim but never the less it was a stupid act.

August 14, is a special day in our lives, it is Ann's birthday. To our surprise, our hosts had a cake with her name on it, a happy birthday breakfast and song. Soon we were off to Glace Bay. Most of the day was spent in the Coal Miners Museum as well as going into a real coal mine. The lecture was conducted by a retired miner and the stories he told were from his life experiences. We still had a day to get to North Sydney and catch the ferry to Newfoundland.

The ride from Glace Bay to North Sydney, was a challenge as we rode through highway construction, hills, and heavy traffic and still had to search for the B&B, which was located at the bottom of a steep descent, so steep our brakes were squealing by the time we reached the bottom of the hill. But this was another great find when it comes to B&B's, run by a mother and daughter. Mary, the daughter, had spotted us at Fort Louisbourg the day before and became excited when we rode into the B&B for the night.

Morning came early as we had to catch the ferry to Argentia, a seaport and industrial park, located in the Town of Placentia,

Newfoundland. Our ferry left North Sydney at 5:45 a.m. and we arrived just five minutes before it pulled out to sea. We tied our bicycles down and found our recliners for the day, which did not recline. So, with a little complaining they moved us to regular seating, which did recline. The ferry terminal in Argentia was 8 klms from our hotel. We never considered the time of arrival in Newfoundland. It was 1:00 a.m. and pitch-black dark. Once we rode away from the terminal, there were no street lights, just darkness. The lights on our bicycles were not bright enough to ride in such darkness. Pot holes! You do not know pot holes until you ride from Argentia to Placentia and the Harold Hotel, Ann walked most of the way, as I slowly rode along attempting to stay upright. We did have one thing going for us, a taxi cab. The driver did not have a fare, so he waited at each turn to make sure we were going in the right direction to the Harold Hotel. When we arrived at the hotel, everything was in high gear, the owners had waited up for us and did a quick welcome, keys and room. Then they shut down the front desk and we all went off to our rooms to sleep.

Our arrival in Argentia was on August 16 and we had until September 2, to reach St. John's across the Island. We took the 17th of August off, as it was raining and after a full day on a ferry it was nice to just lie around and relax. We found Bell's Restaurant for all our meals in Placentia. On the 18th we rode out of Placentia heading to St. John's. This would be a three-day ride, arriving in St. John's on Saturday, August 21, after riding 1,077 miles from Quebec City to St. John's. We started this ride on June 13, and ended on August 21. We would have twelve days to kill in Newfoundland before flying home to Memphis. So, we rented a car, which we could only drive during the daylight hours because of moose. If we hit a moose, the insurance would not pay for the damage. It was very important information to know when it came to renting a car in Newfoundland. For the next week we toured around Newfoundland by car, during the daylight hours only.

There were plenty of things to do in St. John's, with art museums and research centers to visit. The research center had a section of a river with a glass wall so anyone standing there could see how big fish feed on smaller fish! This happened as we were standing by the glass when suddenly a large fish darted through the water and swallowed a smaller fish. There was a group of school children standing with us when it happened, and they became hysterical to the point of screaming!

With a car, we drove to Cape Spear, the most eastern point in North America, also to New Pelican to see another nesting spot for the northern gannet. When we saw them on Bonaventure Island, they were only small chicks, these were now full grown birds being feed by their parents. The noise and smell were the same as when we saw them as young chicks.

That evening we checked into the Old Mill B&B. When we began to boil water for our dinner of freeze-dried food, our landlady almost exploded, "The cod boats are in, go down on the dock and get some fresh cod for your supper." We drove down and looked for a cod boat to purchase the cod, we met David and Irene Perry. They lived in Deep Harbor, Newfoundland, a 26-hour trip by boat to their fishing grounds. When we asked for the cod, they told us the fish had been weighed, but for us to come back the next day and he would save us some fresh cod. During the day, Ann and I found wild blueberries and picked two large zip lock bags of blueberries, one for us and one for the cod, just in case he would not let us pay for the cod. He saw us coming the next day and held up the cod, and said, "I have your fillets." I held up the blueberries and said, "I have your blueberries." The exchange was made and everyone was pleased with the swap.

The next day we drove the car all day around Newfoundland looking for wild life, caribou and elk but no moose. That evening we spent at the Heavenly Hill B&B and stayed on the road most of the next three days. When we returned to St. John's, we were told the best places to eat were located on St. George Street. It turned out to be all tourists, drunks, and people down on their luck. The place was like a dead or dying Overton Square in Memphis, Tennessee.

On September 2, we arrived at the St. John's airport at 4:00 a.m. to catch our flight home to Memphis. The check in did not take long, and we had a pocketful of croissants from the hotel and coffee from the airport. At 6:00 a.m. we departed St. John's and arrived in Newark, NJ at 7:30 a.m. and Memphis at 1:00 p.m., home at last after traveling by bicycle for over three months. The trees around our house were full of windchimes, and our bed had been short sheeted, but there was a steak dinner in the refrigerator. I cooked the steak, corn on the cob, salad, strawberries, and ice cream were also furnished for our welcome home party.

We rode 1,077 miles across Canada and enjoyed every wet, cold, clear, sunny, rainy day and yes, we would do it again! Get a bicycle and travel, ride across any country in the world and the people will ask you a million questions about your travels and you will always be blessed!

2005 Germantown to Pierre, SD
June 19, 2005

Sunday morning and we were riding to Germantown Presbyterian Church when Tom Cates stopped us and asked, "Are you two going to church in those outfits?" "Yes!" We arrived with many laughs as we entered the Little Chapel, listened to the sermon by Don Feuerbach, and then he invited everyone out to the parking lot where our bicycles were parked, and blessed us for our trip to South Dakota.

Our plans for the first day on the ride, were to attend church, visit Suzanne McDearman, and ride to Meeman-Shelby Forest State Park to camp for the night. This we did as we headed north to Covington, and then to Ripley, Tennessee before riding to Reelfoot Lake State Park to camp on our fifth night before crossing into Missouri on the Dorena–Hickman Ferry. It is a ferry crossing the Mississippi River between Dorena, Missouri and Hickman, Kentucky.

Once we entered Missouri, we began to look for a town large enough to have a motel, B&B or lodging of some type. We decided on East Prairie for the night. As we approached East Prairie we spotted a sign for the Grace Inn B&B and decided to check it out, great, very welcoming and clean, also the price was right. The couple running the B&B were about our age, so we had a lot to talk about. The owner, Gary Hancock informed us of a ride the next day named the "Tour-de-Corn."

By this time Ann told me that she was coming down with heat exhaustion. So we went to the local health center and Ann explained to the nurse that she had heat exhaustion. The nurse said that Ann should drink lots of Gator Aid to replace the liquid she had lost. So we bought Gator Aid and returned to the B&B for Ann to recoup.

"Tour de Corn" was on Saturday, and I decided to do the ride while Ann recouped. It was well attended and plenty of fun as there were lots of corn things, corn on the cob and plenty of food along the ride as the route took the riders through lots of corn fields. East Prairie is the Sweet Corn Capital of the United States. After telling Ann about the ride we talked about returning in 2006 to ride the "Tour de Corn" together.

With Ann still under the weather, we asked about staying another night. "Fine, but you will be on your own for breakfast as we are going out of town to church, but you can use our truck to drive to Sikeston for breakfast." With Ann still feeling sick, we decided to go to the Sikeston Hospital to the emergency room and have a doctor check her for heat exhaustion. When we arrived at the hospital, they took x-rays of her chest, and checked her vital signs. All this time she was explaining that she had heat exhaustion. When the doctor came into the room she again explained her condition to him, "I have heat exhaustion." "No ma'am you have pneumonia."

We were stunned! We had been riding for six days from Germantown, Tennessee to East Prairie, Missouri. In six hours our host from the B&B drove us back home. We promised each other never to have our bicycles or our trip blessed again, no matter how high the preacher or religious leader was ranked in God's eyes! Later that year we flew to China and joined thirteen bicyclists from California to ride across southern China.

2005 Across southern China

China, where else could a person ride a bicycle with a billion other people? Ann and I, along with thirteen other bicyclists began our bicycle trip by train from Hong Kong to Guangdong and then by bus to Zhaoqing in Guangdong Provence. We represented Tennessee. All the other bicyclists were from California. In Zhaoqing, we checked into the Song Tao Hotel on the shore of Star Crags Lake. Our Chinese guide, Mr. Ho brought a fully supported team of drivers for three vehicles, a van, a bus and a cargo truck to haul the bicycles. We were fitted with new Diamondback Topanga or Outlook off-road bicycles and went for a test ride around the lake, about twenty kilometers.

Our first dinner was Cantonese food and then off to the open markets in the town square for a taste of shopping in China. Janie Tibbals and I purchased Rolex watches for 24RMB ($3 US) and after that the group always asked, "Are the watches still running? And what time does the Rolex have?" They seemed to think they were "knock offs" how dare they!

The next morning we were loaded on a bus to go the edge of town to pick up our bicycles for a full day of bicycling. First, the ride was along a very busy interstate type road but at no time did we feel in any danger. The vehicles gave us plenty of room. Our only complaint was the horn blowing. It seemed that the Chinese drive more with their horns than their vehicles. Lunch was a picnic along the highway near an elementary school. As we enjoyed our lunch we were entertained by the students as they recited their lessons. Their lessons were more oral than just reading and writing. We were told all Chinese could read the same characters even though they speak either Cantonese or Mandarin.

We soon learned to say "ni hao" for hello as we rode past the schools the children would call out to us "Hello!" "How do you do?" and "How are you?" and the last question was "How old are you?" We would repeat their questions with "Knee-how! mé me ma?" We always received a smile and lots of laughs and waves from all the people we passed.

Outside of Wuzhou, we were picked up in a village with a small market and plenty of Chinese beer. We learned early on to request beer over wine. That evening there were many children gathering around the bus to take a look at the westerners. Linda Hedgepeth of Santa Barbara, California asked Mr. Ho about buying ice cream for the children and he said, "There are too many children" "No, there are too many Americans on this bus for that to be a problem." The ice cream sold for $1 RMB, about 12 cents US. So do the math, $20 RMB of ice cream would buy twenty ice creams for about $2.50 US. Linda, Susan Tescher and I bought sixty ice cream bars and began to give them out, yes the children came from everywhere but we had plenty of Americans to help and plenty of ice cream to give away. The older children looked out for the younger or shy children and made sure everyone received ice cream. On that day we made friends with about sixty young Chinese children and I feel they will remember the kindness of the bus load of bicyclists from America for a long time to come.

That night we stayed in Wuzhou, the snake capital of China. When we asked Mr. Ho if we were having snake for dinner. He explained that since Sars, the government has frowned on eating snakes, so no snake meat for dinner. Our accommodation was the 4-star Dong Zin Hotel. We stayed in 3 and 4-star hotels. We were told to bring plenty of toilet paper and be prepared for the worst. Not so, we had plenty of toilet paper in each room. We were welcomed with a tray containing toothbrush and paste, combs, razors and shaving cream, shampoo, conditioner, soft shoes and in one hotel we received shower shoes. Everything we needed in the way of toiletries was provided. The toilets were western style except in the rural areas we bicycled through. There the toilet paper we brought came in handy and the toilets were the "foot-plant" style. So when going to China be prepared to see plenty of goods we use in America marked "MADE IN CHINA."

We were riding about 80 km per day, with a few 60 km and one 100 km thrown in for the younger riders. Oh! What the heck, all of the riders were younger than Ann and me. We did ride through several small villages of one or two million people, but with Mr. Ho in the lead we tagged along

close behind. We discovered early in China not to look at the drivers attempting to cut through our pace line. If they saw you looking, then it gave them the right to drive across the string of bicyclists.

At the end of our third day we arrived in Yong An Zhou, a typical Chinese town. A river, a beautiful bridge, plenty of people, and of course another shopping opportunity. That night we stayed in the Yong An Zhou Hotel. The next morning we headed into a mountain area of southern China. Not the type of mountains we have in eastern Tennessee, but stand-alone mountains that we did not have to bicycle over but passed as we rode through orange, persimmon, and pomelo groves, as well as farms drying star anise, and rice.

We also watched the farmers harvest their rice by hand. Ann and I stopped to photograph a family harvesting their rice. It appeared there were at least four generations working in the field. I raised my camera and to my delight they nodded yes, so I chose the oldest lady to photograph first and then I took her sickle and began to cut the rice for her to the smiles and laughter of the others in the field. Ann took my photo when I turned around with my arms full of rice. They were using a thresher with a motor the size of a lawn mower to operate the machine. The bagging was done by hand from the rice bin at the end of the thresher. They offered us tea but having been told not to drink the water or local tea, we declined. I thought the friendship would have been worth taking a drink of their tea until Norma Etzler came down with an upset stomach, after that we all watched our eating and drinking habits a little more closely.

On our fifth day of riding we arrived at Half Moon Rock for lunch and then on to Feng Yu Cave Hotel for the night. That evening we took a tour of Feng Yu Cave, which is the largest cave in Asia. We walked 2.5 km into the cave before catching a boat for 3 km to the end of the cave. From the end of the cave we were given a ride back to the hotel by a monorail. Instructions were posted at the entrance of the cave as to how we were to conduct ourselves in the boat, and the last notice to the guests stated, "The demented and the drunk are not permitted to take on the boat."

As we rode along the Li River, we spotted many reed boats being taken out of the river. The trucks were loaded so heavily it appeared they would topple over from the load. It was a weekend and reminded us of canoe float trips in the USA. They were floating downstream and the boats were being carried back to the starting point for more customers.

When we arrived in Xing Ping to cruise the Li River, we spotted a basketball game taking place on an open-air court behind the restaurant where we were having lunch. This was an organized game with referees, uniforms, spectators, and plenty of cheering. Dust was flying into the air as they dribbled the ball from one end of the dirt court to the other. The Chinese people know Yao Ming and the Houston Rockets, just as the

children of Spain know Pau Gasol and the Memphis Grizzlies. That afternoon we floated the Li River in a cruise type boat and watched fishermen using cormorants to catch fish. We rode 30 km, after the float trip, back to the town of Yangzhou. The town is often compared with Kathmandu, Nepal, and Cusco, Peru. This is truly a beautiful part of China. This was just the beginning of the beauty to come.

    China did not celebrate Halloween. Back in Hong Kong Ann and I had purchased masks for the occasion but we soon learned there would not be an official Halloween in China. I misplaced my wallet and feared I had lost my passport and visa. Ann found the wallet after a long search but feeling like the stupid one, and not wanting to show my face, we wore our masks. I went as the number one stupid husband and she appeared as the number one happy wife. I continued to wear the mask during the day as we rode through the country. In a small village I had the mask on when Ann noticed a young boy about to break into tears from fright, so, off came the mask. Several days later we read in an English newspaper that a disco in Beijing had attempted to celebrate Halloween and the young ladies had fled the disco frightened to tears. The newspaper stated Halloween would probably be one western holiday not to catch on in China.

Our last three days of bicycling were spent in the scenic and hilly terraced areas of the Yao People. When we asked our guide, Mr. Ho, how we would recognize the Yao People he explained, "They are shorter than we are, have darker skin, and they wear costumes." So, from that point on we looked for people waring costumes. For almost 100 km's we rode along the Ling Qu River through terraced rice fields. The further we rode along the river, the deeper the river gorge and then it ended at the Long Sheng Hot Springs Hotel. Along the way we passed many swinging bridges from one side of the canyon to the other and each bridge was higher and longer than the one before. The beauty of the region was in the terraced fields from the bottom of the mountains to the top and the watering systems for their fields would amaze most engineers. The water was taken to the top by a hand or a foot pumping system and them routed from field to field back to the river.

This is the region where we visited a Yao Village. The women of the village danced, sang and demonstrated the length and style of their hair. In turn the men in our group formed a line and sang to the young ladies. I wondered if they understood any of the words of, "Jingle Bells," "She Will Be Coming Around The Mountain," or "Happy Birthday" as we sang off key, but loudly. Then Stu Etzler was chosen from the group of men and taken into a separate room and when he returned he was covered with thick kisses of lip stick, to the laughter of the rest of the bicyclists. Now earlier on the ride, Norma Etzler and I had been chosen from our group and when we returned, we had each married a member of the local tribe of minority people. So I suppose, Stu just got even with Norma and her new husband. We left our new spouses behind as we departed Guilin for Xi'an and Beijing. Go bicycle in China and if possible go with Imagine Tours of Davis, CA.

2008 Great Allegheny Passage Bicycle Path and The C&O Canal tow path

By: J. Roscoe Phillips
Special to The Best Times

Oh! What a great summer! We rode seven hundred and fifteen miles on a bicycle path. Ann and I rode from Pittsburgh, PA to Washington, DC and back to Pittsburgh by way of the Great Allegheny Passage bicycle path and the C&O Canal tow path. We have been bicycling for twenty years and this was our first ride on a bicycle path of any distance in the USA.

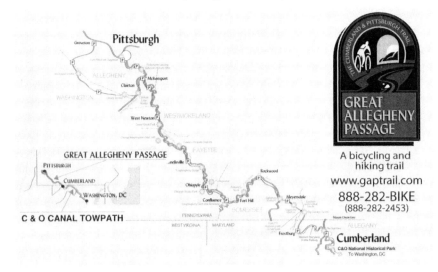

In 2007, while on our way to Ann's class reunion, we stopped to visit Frank Lloyd Wright's "Falling Waters." We had a reservation at the lodge at Ohiopyle State Park, and next to the lodge was a beautiful bicycle path, so we began to inquire about the length of the bike path. To our surprise, we were told that it had just opened all the way from Pittsburgh to Cumberland, Maryland, a distance of 135 miles. We were also told that the trail connected to the C&O Canal tow path, which is also a bicycle path into Washington, DC, another 185 miles. Since we were then in our seventies, we did not have time to revisit places we have been. The Great Allegheny Passage and C&O Canal tow path became our destination for a bicycle ride in 2008.

We began our research for the ride on the internet, through bicycle clubs, B&B's, and magazines before we settled on the direction and final destination. We wanted to spend time riding the trails and still have time to visit Washington as well as Pittsburgh. Since I am an art major with a concentration in graphic art, I wanted to visit all the art museums in both cities. Ann, had never been to Washington and wanted to see it all. Neither of us had been to Pittsburgh and had our eyes set on seeing as much of the city as time would allow.

Our other concern was where to leave our car and in which direction should we ride, east to west first or west to east. West to east won out, as we found a place in Boston, PA to leave our car for the month that we would be riding along the trails. Yough Shore Inn in Boston, PA, agreed to keep our car during the time we would be gone to Washington and return. The Yough Inn is located about two blocks from the Great Allegheny Passage. The owner of the B&B welcomed us upon arrival and showed us where to park our car for the month. We unpacked the car, put the bicycles together, loaded the panniers for the ride and you guessed it, it began to rain.

It rained most of the night and we awakened to the sound of thunder and to the sight of lightning. We have ridden in rain, but lightning is a different subject when it comes to bicycling. We look at ourselves as human lightning rods and that is not the way we want to be remembered. We delayed our start that morning until the storm had passed. We had planned a short ride on the first day, so we started about 10 a.m. and rode to West Newton. We had a reservation at the Bright Morning B&B and arrived just as the rain returned, nice timing. That would be the end of the rain until our arrival in Cumberland, Maryland, five days later. Along our route we met bicyclists, hikers, day trippers, and whole families traveling from Cumberland to Pittsburgh by bicycle.

People ask us, how do we manage enough clothing, food and camping gear as we travel? All I can say is that after twenty years of lists and more lists of what to bring we manage somehow to have plenty of clothing for most all occasions. Food is available in any town in the United States and there are plenty of towns along most trips. The tent always comes

along as an insurance policy, just in case we arrive in a town and cannot find a place to stay. Most of our travel is done without reservations and we have almost, not always, but almost always found a place to stay.

On this ride, we had made a reservation at a B&B just off the C&O. As we rode toward the B&B, Ann discovered a cat just standing on the side of the road. She stopped, as she is a cat lover, the cat walked over to her bicycle and hopped upon her front pannier, sat down and waited for her to ride. It sat, she rode and when we arrived at the B&B, the owner was standing on his porch, he called to the cat, "What are you doing, we have been looking for you all day?" Then he explained the cat was his and had been out hunting, and needed a ride home, so Ann provided the ride. We all laughed and enjoyed the cat.

Camping is a great treat for us when the weather is clear and the nights are cool. On this trip we found camping along the C&O Canal a pleasure. The C&O Canal runs along the

Potomac River. Preserving America's colorful Canal era and transportation history, the Chesapeake & Ohio Canal National Historical Park is 184.5 miles of adventure. Originally, the C&O Canal was a lifeline for communities and businesses along the Potomac River as coal, lumber, grain and other agricultural products floated down the canal to market. Today millions of visitors hike or bike the C&O Canal each year to enjoy the natural, cultural and recreational opportunities available. It is a national park with camp grounds every four to eight miles each with a table, fire ring, port-a-potty and water pump. The park service checks the condition of the wells often and if the water tests unsafe, the park service removes the handles from the pumps.

We began to do our homework long before we arrived in Washington, planning our visits to the many memorials, museums and art galleries. The first thing on our list was to make arrangements to see the Capitol and that only took an e-mail to Senator Bob Corker. We received a phone call from Ms. Davenport, an assistant in his office, and we were given a time to appear at the Senator's office. We were treated royally by Ms. Davenport and moved to the head of many lines to get inside the Capitol. The tour lasted about two hours with her leading the way and explaining the many features of the building to us as we moved through the large crowd. I asked Ms. Davenport how many people she had escorted through the Capitol since Senator Corker had arrived in Washington and she stated, "I have escorted about 3,000 Republicans through since his arrival." When I announced she had now escorted one old Democrat, she fell silent and escorted us to the Senate floor where she announced her departure and we were left to roam through the Capitol alone. "Thank you Senator Corker, and Ms. Davenport for the hospitality you showed us in Washington."

While in Washington, we walked, rode the subway, bus and shared a taxi with a British couple who felt so sorry for two people in the U.S. who had to travel by bicycle to Washington, that they picked up the cab fare. Our tour took us to all the wonderful memorials and of course we visited Arlington National Cemetery. We watched the changing of the guard, the changing of the wreath and then someone down the way dropped a camera lens cap. The guard stopped, marched to the guard house and called for assistance. It was just as if the changing of the guard took place all over again and the lens cap was retrieved. The guard held up the lens cap when he exited the grave site but no one admitted to being the person who dropped the lens cap. We had a good laugh and so did the soldier who held the lens cap.

Other places we visited in Washington were the Old Postal Building, which has one of the best views of Washington, took a look at the White House from all sides, the Lincoln Memorial, World War II, Korean War, Air and Space Museum and the Washington Monument. The museums included the National Art Museum, Hirschhorn Museum and Sculpture Garden, and The Phillips Collection.

Upon our return to Pittsburgh we visited the Carnegie Mellon Art Facility, Andy Warhol and Clayton House Museums before enjoying a ride on the Duquesne Incline Railroad. If you have not visited Pittsburgh, I think you will be pleasantly surprised, for it is a hidden jewel.

We rode a total of 715 miles and only two blocks of it was in Washington traffic because we rode up Rock Creek Bicycle Trail to Kennedy Street to the International Guest House. On the two trails, we had a six mile detour each way on the C&O Canal because of a washout on the trail during a flood several years ago. To ride the trail visit The Great Allegheny Passage on the web at www.atatrail.org/. The C&O Canal is a national park and anyone interested in visiting the park should visit their web site at www.nps.gov/choh/ and have a great ride.

2010 Katy Trail across Missouri

We rented a car, carried our bicycles and panniers to the start of our ride from Independence, Missouri to Germantown, Tennessee. After two days of visiting the home of Harry S. Truman and the Truman library. We loaded our bicycles and headed home on Wednesday, May 26. We rode 55 miles, from Independence to Warrensburg, and stayed in the Days Inn Warrensburg. The next day was a short 38 miles from Warrensburg to Sedalia, and we camped at the Missouri State Fairgrounds and the western end of the Katy Trail across Missouri.

The Katy Trail is a 268-mile-long state park across Missouri. The Katy Trail State Park is the country's longest recreational rail trail. It runs along the northern bank of the Missouri River, in the right-of-way of the former Missouri–Kansas–Texas Railroad. It is open year-round from sunrise to sunset, and serves hikers, joggers, and bicyclists. It has a hard, flat surface of "limestone pug" (crushed limestone). The limestone dust did a number on our gears and derailleurs, and cleaning them each day became a real chore. We rode the trail on 24 mm tires.

On Friday, we rode 38 miles, from Sedalia to Boonville, and another 38 miles, Boonville to Hartsburg. In Hartsburg we found the Katy Rest Caboose, which served as an overnight stop and worked as a "room in the inn" type of place to stay the night. On Sunday, it was 43 miles, from Hartsburg to Bluffton, and camping at the Steamboat Junction Campground. We camped again on May 31, after a 35-mile ride from Bluffton to Marthasville, and camped at the Community Club Park. Our last day on the trail was from Marthasville to St.. Charles, where we rented a cabin at the Sundermeier RV park for three days, rented a car in Marthasville, and visited St.. Louis. This was a total of 298 miles from Independence, Missouri to the outskirts of St. Louis.

After reaching St. Louis, our trip turned south on the Mississippi River Trail for our return trip to Germantown and home. We started south on Friday, June 4, and rode 58 miles from St.. Louis to Pevely. June 5, Saturday, 42 miles, Pevely to Ste Genevieve, and on June 6, Sunday, Day off in Ste Genevieve. On June 7, Monday, 24 miles, Ste Genevieve to Perryville and on June 8, Tuesday, 47 miles from Perryville to Cape Girardeau and 52 miles, Cape Girardeau to Charleston, and June 10, Thursday, 46 miles, Charleston to Reelfoot Lake State Park. We had planned to continue our trip home but the temperature climbed to over 100°s and with Ann's record of heat related ills, we decided to ask for a ride.

We have always found help along our rides for camping, or places to stay inside when the weather turned bad. This was one of those times. When we asked our server at Boyette's Dining Room in Reelfoot, if she knew anyone with a pick-up truck we could hire to drive us home, she said, "I am driving to Memphis in the morning and you are welcome to come along for the ride, I'll pick you up in the morning." She did and we ended our trip from Independence at Reelfoot Lake State Park. We rode 365 miles and came up short by 107 miles of our goal of 472 miles.

Hudson River Valley, 2013
July 30 to August 2, 2013

We met our tour in Albany, New York. Ann and I drove from Germantown, TN to Albany with all our gear as well as our bicycles. Since this was a fully supported ride we had to pack carefully with our clothing and camping gear as they would be delivered to the campsite at the end of each day's ride. We arrived on July 29, and camped at Sage College as we prepared for the ride from Albany to the Battery in New York City. We would leave our car at Sage College and the tour would shuttle us back to Albany after the ride. This was a six-day ride, with a day off in Hyde Park to visit President Franklin D. Roosevelt's library. Also, along the route we camped at Saint Basil Academy in Garrison, across from West Point. With another day off, we rode to West Point, and were escorted around the Academy by a retired General, who just happened to be on the tour.

Our tour started on a Monday from Albany to Hudson, a distance of 40 miles with camping on the campus of Columbia Greene Community College. From Hudson, another 42 miles to Hyde Park where we camped at Regina Coeli Catholic School. With a couple days off and a reservation at the Culinary Institute of America where we enjoyed an evening of French dining. The dress code for the Culinary Institute of America was business casual, no jacket required. With a short bus ride we arrived in our foul weather gear and one of the ladies on the bus informed us we would not be allowed to eat at the Institute. Little did she know I had explained to the person taking our reservation that all we had was bicycle clothing plus the rain gear. We were told they would make an exception for us as we were on the bicycle tour. When we headed to the desk to check in the "informer" was standing in the hall waiting to see the disappointment on our faces when we were turned away. As we were led toward our table, I smiled at her and received a very disgusted look as we were being seated. I felt like a big, "Ha Ha" was in store for our accomplishment in being seated right in front of the nay-sayer.

During the day off, we visited the Roosevelt Museum, library, and Eleanor's house. We rode around Hyde Park and enjoyed the day off. On August 1, we rode 53 miles to Garrison, and 12.5 miles to West Point and another 12.5 to return to Garrison. Before riding 27 miles to Nyack and camping at Nyack Beach State Park on Rockland Lake.

The last day was 32 miles of near panic as we crossed the George Washington Bridge into Manhattan, ending at Battery Park. When I stated near panic, it seemed pace lines were the way to travel across the Bridge. We have ridden across a lot of famous bridges, even the Golden Gate and nothing prepared us for the ride across the George Washington Bridge. There is only one side of the bridge for bicyclists, in both directions.

Now add pace lines riding at breakneck speed and it is almost impossible to keep cool and not get into an accident. This was an experience I do not hope to reenact anytime soon. The ride to the Battery was easy as the bike path is wide and divided with lines separating the two directions.

This ride is sponsored by Parks and Trails of New York. They also sponsor the Erie Canal ride and others. It is a state supported ride each year and well attended.

Rhine Bike Path: Mainz to Cologne, 2015

Tour Description: Self-guided

The Rhine Bike Path from Mainz to Cologne is along the most beautiful part of the river. The hot springs and spas attracted the ancient Romans to the Rhine. Today vineyards and picturesque towns add to the region's charm.

We admired the gorgeous landscapes as we rode to Cologne, where you can see the cathedral spires tower over Germany's oldest city and enjoy its innumerable cultural and historical treasures, world-famous museums and active art scene. Life in Cologne is uncomplicated and vivacious. It's a wonderful town for the end of a fabulous tour.

This will be our last long-distance ride as age is taking its toll. We will ride short day trips or drive to a destination for day rides but probably never another long-distance trip on a loaded bicycle and never on a camping trip cross country. We will miss this type of travel.

We flew into Cologne, and took the high-speed train to Frankfurt, and a local to Mainz. Oh! Wait a minute we caught the local to Mainz and about halfway the train stopped, made an announcement and everyone stood up and began to depart the train. We began to ask what had happened, of course in English, no replies, then a young lady said "Stay on the train it is returning to Frankfurt." I continued to ask what was going on and finally she said "Someone has committed suicide by sitting on the track ahead of this train and we will be sent on another train to Mainz if we stay on this one as it will return to Frankfurt." We did and soon arrived back in Frankfurt, caught another train and arrived later in Mainz. That was the last of the excitement for that day.

Day 1: We could see the hotel as we departed the train but that did not stop the cab drivers from attempting to load our gear into their cabs for the trip across the street to the hotel Konigshof. We began to laugh and pointed to the hotel.

Day 2 and 3 were spent in Mainz. Our bicycles were rented from the tour company and delivered to our hotel, one ladies 21 speed and one men's 21 speed. They had been built by the Panzer Tank Company, well maybe not, but our bicycles back home weigh in at 24 pounds, these would weigh in at 40 to 50 pounds easily, but with 21 gears and German engineering they were easy riders. We also did all the tourist things during our two day stay in Mainz. The 1000-year old cathedral, the Gutenberg museum, the Catholic Church St. Stephan with nine unique windows designed by Marc Chagall, and the picturesque historic district were only a few of Mainz' beautiful sights.

For several years I taught typography at Southwest Tennessee Community College. My dream was to go to Mainz, visit the Gutenberg Museum and operate the press. I had been told that during the exhibit they would demonstrate the Gutenberg Press, and if you volunteered to help they would let you print on the press. I would love to have been the chosen one, but I did not understand the German language and missed the opportunity to volunteer to be the press helper, so I did not get to operate the Gutenberg Press. I watched as a member of the audience stepped up to take the job.

Day 4: Saturday, July 25 Mainz - Rüdesheim (19-31 mi/35-49 km) This was the first day of our ride on the Rhine toward Cologne. We began to wonder if we had picked the correct direction to ride as we had a headwind that almost stopped us as we rode down the Rhine. The beautiful first stage lead us through rolling vineyards and well-known wine villages. The Rhine flows unhurriedly, forming little islands and broadening its bed up to a width of 2600 ft/800 m. before we reached Rüdesheim for our overnight stay.

Day 5: Sunday, July 26 Rüdesheim - St. Goar (24 mi/38 km) We passed grand castles along today's route. You definitely should climb up to the Loreley! A hiking path leads up to this lovely spot and offers a beautiful view of the narrowest part of the romantic Rhine Valley.

Day 6: Monday, July 27 St. Goar - Koblenz (22 mi/36 km) Further on in the narrow Rhine Valley, the route took us to a cable car station and a ride to the top of the Rhine Gorge. Upon arriving in Koblenz we discovered a medieval reenactment at the Castle Marksburg. So we took a day off to enjoy the reenactment in Koblenz. That was day 7.

Day 8: Wednesday, July 29 Koblenz -Bad Godesberg (36 mi/58 km) This was our first encounter with the thermal baths along the Rhine, and to take time to enjoy the beer gardens. We also took a break from cycling and enjoyed a boat trip on the Rhine. Between Koblenz and Bad Godesberg! Overnight in Bad Godesberg was spent in a spa hotel with the thermal baths.

Day 9: Thursday, July 30 Bad Godesberg - Cologne (27 mi/43 km) We planned to visit Bonn from Cologne as we were staying in Cologne for a couple days before heading home. Our hotel in Cologne was a well-kept secret as we had to search for the street to the hotel, many phone calls and lots of misunderstood directions before we arrived at the correct hotel.

On Saturday we caught the train to Bonn, and what a surprise! It was packed wall-to-wall with only a few empty seats. We were lucky, and able to squeeze into a group seating of people in costumes. Yes, costumes, not bicycle clothes as we have been asked, "You travel in those costumes?" These were costumes of cartoon characters from the Japanese cartoons. They were having a festival in Bonn and we were riding along to enjoy Bonn and whatever there was to see at the festival.

On our return to Cologne, the train was packed again. As we entered one of the passenger cars, I spotted an open seat and pushed Ann into the seat and told her I would look for a seat in back of the car. As I walked a couple rows back, a gentleman motioned me to take the seat across from him. This was on the narrow side of the car, so only two people faced each other and we began to talk. Being shy as I am, I told him about our bicycle trip along the Rhine. When the train started and everyone was quiet, the man seated across from Ann began to talk very loudly, louder, and even louder. He sounded as if he were lecturing or upset about something. I began to worry, so I asked the gentleman across from me, "What is going on?" He asked, "Does your wife speak German?" "No, what is he talking about, religion or politics?" "No, he is talking German." All I could do was smile as I almost broke into open laughter. He did not understand what I had asked. The ranting continued for quite a while before he figured out that Ann did not understand him and he stopped his rant.

When we returned to our hotel, we checked our bicycles into the tour company, and made plans for the trip to the airport the next day. We were looking forward to coming home. Then we had those sad thoughts, was this the last long-distance ride?

Since 2015
Mississippi Bicycle Paths

We are still on our bicycles as often as we can be depending on the weather. Also we have discovered several bicycle paths of forty miles or more to ride. One of the most enjoyable of these is the Tanglefoot Trail.

The Tanglefoot Trail is a 43.5-mile trail located near New Albany, Mississippi that features a river and is good for all skill levels. We have enjoyed an overnight stay in Pontotoc, Mississippi, because we ride north to New Albany, one day and then south to Houston the next day, Ponotoc is about halfway between the two towns and a good day's ride of forty miles each day. Just south of Ponotoc is the largest sheep ranch in Mississippi. The sheep can be heard long before you arrive to enjoy the sight. The trail crosses several rivers and streams as it rolls through the Mississippi countryside.

Another Mississippi trail is the Longleaf Trace. The Longleaf Trace is a 41-mile (66 km) paved pedestrian, equestrian, rollerblade, and bicycle trail located between Hattiesburg and Prentiss, Mississippi. The Trace was constructed in 2000. It follows a portion of the abandoned Mississippi Central Railroad line. It has nine stations along its route (Prentiss, Ed Parkman Road, Carson, Bassfield, Lott Circle, Sumrall, Epley, Clyde Depot, Jackson Road). Trail access is from public road access points only, located an average of 5 miles (8.0 km) apart. The following roads hold a rest stop and parking lot accessing the Trace. In Hattiesburg: University of Southern Mississippi, West 4th street and Jackson Road. We have driven to Prentiss and stayed overnight, then we rode out and back on the Trace. Along this route the Trace passes an exotic animal farm, llamas, emus, ostrich, chickens, pigs, miniature horses, sheep and cows, lots of animals to watch as you ride the Trace.

Arkansas Bicycle Paths
The Razorback Greenway

In 2018 we were the guests of the State of Arkansas to introduce the opening of the Northwest Arkansas Razorback Greenway. They say nice things happen to nice people; I suppose we must be nice as we were treated to a wonderful weekend as we traveled the new Razorback Greenway. It begins in Fayetteville and ends in Bella Vista. We took our time on the ride and enjoyed all the offerings from the Arkansas Tourist Bureau. We arrived in Fayetteville for our first night's stay with a member of the PEO. The P.E.O. Sisterhood (Philanthropic Educational Organization) is a U.S.-based international women's organization of about 230,000 members, with a primary focus on providing educational opportunities for female students worldwide. Since Ann is a member of the Sisterhood, and supporting education by raising funds for education through a B&B system we found a B&B in Fayetteville for a couple days.

After a couple days with her Sister, we loaded our bicycles and rode from Fayetteville to Rogers, Arkansas. At this point the Arkansas Tourist Bureau, put us up in a local hotel and set up a meeting the next day with a local television crew. We were filmed, interviewed, wined, and dined as guests of the state of Arkansas. The next day we rode from Rogers to Bentonville for a two-night stay in a wonderful B&B. The bicycle path was not an old railroad trail, it had great climbs and wonderful paybacks along the trail. So again I encourage you to travel to Fayetteville and enjoy the Razorback Greenway.

In Little Rock, The Big Dam Loop bicycle path runs from downtown Little Rock west along the Arkansas River to the Murray Lock and Dam and crosses the dam on the Big Dam Bridge over the Arkansas River to the north side and the trail returns to North Little Rock along the Arkansas River for 14 miles of scenic riverside trails.

Experience the longest pedestrian and bicycle bridge in North America, built specifically for that use. This impressive structure was named the Big Dam Bridge because of its massive 4,226-foot span built atop Murray Lock and Dam.

Elevated up to 90 feet above the Arkansas River, the Big Dam Bridge connects over 14 miles of scenic riverside trails in the cities of Little Rock and North Little Rock, and assists in the connection of 70,000 acres of various city, county, state and federal park land. It's one of several Little Rock bridges that serve bicyclists and pedestrians. The trail provides cyclist and pedestrian access to the Clinton Presidential Center, the River Market, museums, and restaurants.

Big River Crossing, Mississippi River

opened in 2016

At nearly a mile in length, Big River Crossing is the longest public pedestrian bridge across the Mississippi River. Big River Crossing is also the country's longest active rail/bicycle/pedestrian bridge. It serves as the connection point of Main Street to Main Street, a 10-mile, multi-modal corridor that also features the Big River Trail System, creating ties to attractions throughout the Memphis, West Memphis, and delta region. Construction began in 2014 and took two years to complete, opening in 2016 to the public.

Since that time Ann and I have ridden our bicycles across the bridge many times, but the most enjoyable rides are the ones ending at Poncho's Restaurant in West Memphis. One such ride was a morning ride, arriving at Poncho's in time for lunch. We had invited Suzanne McDearman to join us on the ride, so marguerites were ordered. And the ride back across the bridge was even more fun, with plenty of laughs. This gave Ann and me the idea to ride to Poncho's for dinner and stay over-night in West Memphis before returning home the next day. So, we did, with a light load of overnight clothing, we headed out on a Saturday morning for the thirty-three-mile one-way ride. This would make the trip a total of sixty-six miles for two days.

From our home in Germantown, we rode the Green-way Bicycle path to Shelby Farms Park, across the park and then on to the Green-Line path to Overton Park before riding on the streets to connect to the River-trail and on to the Big River Crossing and a bicycle path into West Memphis. We stopped on Broadway Ave. at the Bounty Restaurant for lunch on our way to West Memphis. Once we approached Poncho's we began to look for a place to stay the night within walking distance of Poncho's. With laughs, we chose the Crown Plaza Inn, checked in for the night, walked to Poncho's for dinner and then returned for a quiet night of sleep. WRONG! We did not know the West Memphis Dirt Track was behind the Crown Plaza Inn. About 8:00 p.m. the races began, loud race cars, really loud race cars for hours. Then about 11:00 o'clock the races stopped, now we could sleep, no, they took a break and began anew. Now the racing continued until 1:00 a.m. and stopped, great we could sleep. NO! Now the audience would start their trek out of the park, each car, truck or type of transportation leaving the race was louder than the other and this would take another hour for them to exit the parking lot. Now we could sleep! No! Not yet as the people who had attended the races were now racing up and down in front of the Crown Plaza Inn.

Ann and I are retired, we can ride on any day of the week and we are still asking ourselves, why on a Saturday night? The ride was wonderful, the dinner was great, the bed was soft, and the place was close to Poncho's but it was also close to the "Dirt Track." Our return trip was at a much faster pace than our trip to West Memphis, and a nap was waiting for us upon arriving home. We are getting older and our trips are taking a toll on our bodies. This was our last ride to an overnight destination, at this time.

The Wrap-up of many years of Bicycling!

Ann and I started our life together in 1989. We met on a 150-mile ride to raise money for MS (National Multiple Sclerosis Society). The stories in this book are recounts of the many bicycle rides we have taken since that time. Also the many wonderful laughs we have had as we encountered people along the way. And, I hope I have expressed our gratitude to all the people who helped us. Life just got better as we created new friendships. We are always surprised by the many Christmas cards we still receive each year from the friends we made as we traveled.

I hope you enjoyed the stories but most of all, I hope I have inspired you to travel by bicycle. When you do travel by bicycle, and ride into a town on a loaded bicycle, panniers hanging on your bicycle, people always want to know how far you have ridden your bicycle loaded "like that." It is so much fun to feel you have accomplished something very few people have ever attempted.

   It would be wonderful to list the many companies that helped us on our rides, but all you need to do is use the internet to find plenty of resources for traveling by bicycle. Also with the changing world and the uncertainty of how companies will survive during this pandemic, it would be best to let you do your own research into bicycle travel companies. Of course, there is one company I feel I need to give a huge shout out to, and that is Adventure Cycling of Missoula, Montana and also to Cycle America. They can both be found on the internet, so check them out. We traveled using the maps from Adventure Cycling and we rode the Washington section with Cycle America. Other touring companies included, Imagine Tours, which is owned by Nancy Redpath. We did three tours with Nancy, one in the USA, one in Canada and a one across China in 2005. The state of Tennessee has a yearly ride called BRAT, (Bicycle Ride Across Tennessee). There are other state rides supported by the different state tourist departments. They are a very good way to start touring as they are supported and you will not have to carry your luggage, just learn to pack for a bicycle trip.

   I hope you are now inspired to purchase a "Touring Bike," not a mountain bike to ride on trips. Here is why, friction, yes, the more tire that hits the road the more you will have to peddle your bicycle. So, get a very good touring bike. I recommend 24 mm tires with a 120 psi and see just how far you can roll along without peddling. Next you will need the best panniers you can afford, four, two on the front wheel and two on the rear. This will give you plenty of room for clothing, camping gear, and accessories. Now you are ready for that shake-down ride. Ride to your local or state park where you can camp for the night, cook dinner, breakfast and then return home, just keep a record of what you needed that you did not have with you. Enjoy and travel by bicycle!

The Appendix: appendix AA

Adventure Cycling Association
Adventure Cycling Association is a nonprofit member organization focused on travel by bicycle. Headquartered in Missoula, Montana, Adventure Cycling develops cycling routes, publishes maps, provides guided trips, and advocates for better and safer cycling in the U.S.

> **Listed below are the map numbers and names:
> First the Northern Tier Route from 1999
> Second the TransAmerica Trail from 2001**

Northern Tier (west to east 1999)
Anacortes, WA to Bar Harbor, ME
11 Map Set (4294.0 mi.)
1. Anacortes, WA to Sandpoint, ID (457.5 mi.)
2. Sandpoint, ID to Cut Bank, MT (444.9 mi.)
3. Cut Bank, MT to Dickinson, ND (567.3 mi.)
4. Dickinson, ND to Fargo, ND (343.5 mi.)
5. Fargo, ND to Walker, MN (173.7 mi.)
10. Orchard Park, NY to Ticonderoga, NY (426.5 mi.)
11. Ticonderoga, NY to Bar Harbor, ME (437.2 mi.)

TransAmerica Trail (west to east 2001)
Astoria, OR to Yorktown, VA
12 Map Set (4215.2 mi.)
1. Astoria, OR to Coburg, OR
2. Coburg, OR to Baker City, OR
3. Baker City, OR to Missoula, MT
4. Missoula, MT to West Yellowstone, MT
5. West Yellowstone, MT to Rawlins, WY
6. Rawlins, WY to Pueblo, CO
7. Pueblo, CO to Alexander, KS
8. Alexander, KS to Girard, KS
9. Girard, KS to Murphysboro, IL
10. Murphysboro, IL to Berea, KY
11. Berea, KY to Christiansburg, VA
12. Christiansburg, VA to Yorktown, VA

"Cycling The Netherlands, Belgium, and Luxembourg"
By: Katherine and Jerry Whitehill, 1998
Pages 89 and 90 Route 2 (SN1)

Part I: **"France by Bike"**
Part II: **"14 Tours Geared for Discovery"**
by: Karen and Terry Whitehill
A list of Tours in the order we rode them:
Tour No. 4, Tour No. 11, Tour No. 5, Tour No. 3, Tour No. 2, and Tour No. 1
We returned to France in 2001 and completed many of the other tours in "France by Bike."

"Ireland By Bicycle"
second edition
21 Tours Geared for Discovery
By: Robin Krause

Palatino

Palatino is the name of an old-style serif typeface designed by Hermann Zapf, and used for the text in this book. It was initially released in 1949 by the Stempel foundry and later by other companies, most notably the Mergenthaler Linotype Company.

Hermann Zapf (November 8, 1918 – June 4, 2015) was a German type designer and calligrapher who lived in Darmstadt, Germany. He was married to the calligrapher and typeface designer Gudrun Zapf-von Hesse. Zapf's career in type design spanned the three most recent stages of printing: hot metal composition, phototypesetting, and digital typesetting. His two most famous typefaces, Palatino and Optima, were designed in 1948 and 1952. Palatino was designed in conjunction with August Rosenberger, with careful attention to detail. It was named after the 16th-century Italian writing master Giambattista Palatino. Zapf intended the design to bridge serifs and sans serifs and to be suitable for both headings and continuous passages of text.